Making PEACE

Karyn Henley

Standard
PUBLISHING

CINCINNATI, OHIO

Making **PEACE**

The foundation for living in fellowship

Karyn Henley

FOUNDATIONS
CURRICULUM

© 2002 Karyn Henley
All rights reserved
Exclusively administered by Child Sensitive Communication, LLC

Published by Standard Publishing, Cincinnati, Ohio
A division of Standex International Corporation

Credits
Cover design by Brian Fowler
Interior design by Jeff Richardson
Cover and inside illustrations by Ed Koehler
Project editors: Ruth Frederick, Bruce E. Stoker

08 07 06 05 04 03 02   5 4 3 2 1
ISBN 0-7847-1369-3
Printed in the United States of America

TABLE OF CONTENTS

INTRODUCTION

The Irish poet William Butler Yeats once said, "Education is not the filling of a pail, but the lighting of a fire." In the first temple, the tent of meeting, there was a lampstand. God's instructions were, "Tell the people of Israel to bring you pure olive oil for the lampstand, so it can be kept burning continually. . . . Aaron and his sons will keep the lamps burning in the Lord's presence day and night" (Exodus 27:20, 21, NLT). Today we are God's temple (1 Corinthians 3:16). And our passion, our living love for the Lord, keeps our lamp burning before him. (See Revelation 2:4, 5.) Our job in the spiritual education of children is to light a fire, a living, growing love for God within them.

The Foundations curriculum can help light that fire. Each of our students is a temple of God. The goal of the Foundations curriculum is to construct within children the essential foundations upon which they can build (and sustain) a loving, thriving relationship with God. To do this, the Foundations curriculum provides a thorough, step-by-step, systematic exploration of the following foundations.

Quarter 1: Studying the Bible, The Foundation for Knowing God

Quarter 2: Salvation, The Foundation for Living with God

Quarter 3: Prayer, The Foundation for Growing Closer to God

Quarter 4: Worship, The Foundation for Loving God

Quarter 5: Lordship, The Foundation for Following God

Quarter 6: Stewardship, The Foundation for Reflecting God

Quarter 7: Missions, The Foundation for Sharing God

Quarter 8: Making Peace, The Foundation for Living in Fellowship

This curriculum is intended for use with students in third through fifth grades. Each quarter is independent of the others, so they can be taught in any order. In fact, each quarter can be used as a single unit to fill in a 13-week study at any time of the year and can be followed or preceded by any other curriculum of your choice.

The following arrangement is a suggestion showing how the Foundations Curriculum can be taught in two years. Studying the Bible (September-November), Salvation (December-February), Prayer (March-May), Worship (June-August), Lordship (September-November), Stewardship (December-February), Missions (March-May), Making Peace (June-August).

WALK THROUGH A WEEK

SCRIPTURE AND GOAL

The session begins with a Scripture and a simple goal. You may use the Scripture as a memory verse if you wish, or you may use it to support the theme for the day, reading the Scripture when you gather for the first prayer.

INTRODUCTORY ACTIVITY

You can begin your introductory activity as soon as the first student arrives, guiding others to join you as they come into your room. This activity serves two purposes. First, it gives the students something fun to do from the first moment they arrive. Second, it starts thoughts and conversations about the theme of the session. Talking is encouraged. Questions are welcome. Get to know your students. Make it your goal to discover something interesting and special about each one. Let them know that their mission is to discover more about God and about how they can get to know him better every day, so that God becomes their constant companion, their treasured friend, their awesome king.

DISCOVERY RALLY

Gather the students together as a group in preparation for the Discovery centers.

What's the Good Word? This is a time to read the Scripture for the day. You may also sing a few songs if you want.

Challenge. This is a time to introduce the students to the theme for the day by making challenging statements or asking challenging questions.

Prayer. Choose a student to lead a prayer of blessing for the day's activities, asking God to open your hearts and teach everyone present.

DISCOVERY CENTERS

You will need either one teacher/facilitator for each center, or clearly written instructions that tell the students what they are to do in the center.

The way your class uses Discovery Centers will depend on how much time you have and how many students there are in your class.

• If you have a few students, go together to as many centers as you can in the time you have.

• If you have more than ten students and lots of time, divide into three groups. Send one group to each center and let each group rotate to a different center as they finish the activity, so that each student gets to go to each center during Discovery Center time.

• If you have more than ten students, but little time, divide into groups of three. Number off, one to three in each group. Each student #1 goes to the first center, #2 goes to the second, #3 goes to the third. After each center has completed its activity, the original groups of three come back together again to tell each other what they learned in their centers.

• Or you may choose to let all three centers do the same activity. Choose the one or two activities that you think your students will enjoy most. Divide the students into groups for centers, and once they are there, do not rotate. Instead, let each group do the one or two activities you have chosen.

DEBRIEFING QUESTIONS

If you have time, gather together as a large group at the end of the session to ask and answer questions and discuss the theme and/or other issues on the students' minds.

Review the Scripture for the day.

PRAY

You or a student may close your class time in prayer.

SUGGESTED BIBLE STUDY HELPS

This is by no means a complete list. As you look for these, you will find others that may be just as interesting and helpful.

Bible Handbooks

What the Bible Is All About, Henrietta C. Mears (Gospel Light)
What the Bible Is All About for Young Explorers, Frances Blankenbaker (Gospel Light)
The International Children's Bible Handbook, Lawrence Richards (Word)
The Baker Bible Handbook for Kids, Marek Lugowski and Carol J. Smith (Baker)
New Unger's Bible Handbook: Student Edition, Merrill Unger (Moody)

Bible Encyclopedias

The Children's Bible Encyclopedia: The Bible Made Simple and Fun, Mark Waters (Baker Books)

Bible Dictionaries

International Children's Bible Dictionary, Lynn Waller (Word)
The Baker Bible Dictionary for Kids (Baker)

Bible Fact Books

The Awesome Book of Bible Facts, Sandy Silverthorne (Harvest House)
The Baker Book of Bible People for Kids (Baker)
The Complete Book of Bible Trivia, J. Stephen Lang (Tyndale)

For Teachers and Older Students

Willmington's Bible Handbook, Harold L. Willmington (Tyndale)
Holman Topical Concordance (Holman Bible Publishers)
Holman Bible Dictionary (Holman Bible Publishers)
Children's Ministry Resource Edition (Thomas Nelson)
Manners and Customs in the Bible, Victor H. Matthews (Hendrickson)

What is Peacemaking?

Scripture

"Do your part to live in peace with everyone, as much as possible." Romans 12:18, NLT

Goal

Learn what it means to make peace.

INTRODUCTION

Hang a six-foot length of butcher paper along a wall at your students' eye level. Draw a vertical line down the middle of the paper. Write "conflict" at the top of the left side of the paper and "peace" at the top of the right side. Have scissors, glue, newspapers, and news magazines available. (You may want to remove any ads or articles that would be offensive.) As students arrive, ask them to look through the newspapers and magazines and cut out photos that depict people who are in conflict: arguing, fighting, worried, stressed, or afraid. They glue those photos in the "Conflict" section of the mural. They can also look for photos that show people at peace. They cut those out and glue them to the "Peace" side of the mural.

DISCOVERY RALLY

Gather the students together in a large group.

WHAT'S THE GOOD WORD?

Choose a student to read the Scripture for the day.

THE CHALLENGE

Ask the students to describe the photos in the conflict section of the mural. Ask: **What is conflict?** Some answers might be: disagreement, tension, arguing, fighting, worry, stress, fear. Ask: **Why do you think some of these people are having conflict?** Then ask students to describe the photos in the peace section of the mural. Ask: **What is peace?** Some answers might be: no worry, stillness, comfort, happiness, quietness, rest. Ask: **Why do you think some of these people are at peace? Which side of the mural would you rather have your photo on? Which photos on this mural show people who could use someone to help them make peace?** Ask students to raise their hands if they've ever experienced or witnessed conflict. Tell the students that for the next few weeks, they will be learning how to become peacemakers. Tell the students that in their Discovery Centers today, they'll learn what peacemaking is.

PRAYER

DISCOVERY CENTERS

1. PEACE ALL AROUND

Before class, copy the Peace All Around page and cut the Scriptures apart. Place each Scripture in an envelope. Then place the envelopes inside each other from smallest to largest so that you end up with one large envelope.

MATERIALS

One copy of Peace All Around (page 14), scissors, eight to ten envelopes of different sizes (from a small gift tag envelope to a very large manila envelope), an audio tape or CD of peaceful music, and a tape or CD player

DO: Seat the students in a circle. Give one of them the envelope. When you start the music, they start passing the envelope around the circle. Stop the music at random. The student holding the envelope opens it. He takes out the Scripture and the second envelope. He reads the Scripture aloud. Then the music starts again, and the second envelope goes around the circle. Continue play until all envelopes have been opened and read.

DISCUSS: Ask: **What did you hear about peace and peacemakers as these verses were read?** Say: **A peacemaker is someone who brings friendship or peace between people who are in conflict with each other. It's even possible to be the peacemaker between yourself and someone else. What might be difficult about peacemaking? Why is peacemaking important? Do people have to agree on everything in order to live peacefully? No. People will never agree on everything, but they can still live at peace with each other.**

2. PEACE FLIP

DO: Give each student a copy of the Peace Flip page. Ask students to cut out the ten pictures. They glue or tape each picture to an index card, with the right edge of the picture near the right edge of the card. Then direct them to fill in the blanks on the pictures as follows:

MATERIALS

one copy for each student of Peace Flip (page 15), scissors, ten index cards for each student, tape or glue, large stapler and staples, pens, a Bible

On picture #2: P in the first blank

#3:	P in the first blank, E in the second blank
#4:	P E A
#5:	P E A C
#6:	P E A C E
#7:	P E A C E M
#8:	P E A C E M A
#9:	P E A C E M A K
#10:	P E A C E M A K E R

Students stack their cards with #10 on the bottom and #1 on the top. Staple the left edges together. Now they hold the book and flip the pages with their thumb.

DISCUSS: Ask: **What does it mean to "make peace"?** Say: **A peacemaker is someone who brings friendship or peace between people who are in conflict with each other.** Ask someone to read Isaiah 9:6. Ask: **Who is this verse talking about? Why is Jesus called the Prince of Peace?** Remind the students of the Scripture for today. Ask: **Why does God want us to live at peace with each other? Does living at peace mean we all have to agree on everything? How can you live at peace if you disagree on something? Is it always possible to live at peace with everyone? Why or why not?**

3. PLACE OF PEACE

MATERIALS

manila paper, crayons, watercolor markers, a Bible

DO: Give each student a piece of manila paper. Ask them to think of the most peaceful place they like to be. It may even be a hidden secret place where they go to be alone. Or it may be a place where there are peaceful, joyful people around. Ask them to draw that place. If they can't think of a place, ask them to draw a place that they think would be the most peaceful place for them to go. Ask them to write "Jesus: Prince Of Peace" at the top of the picture.

DISCUSS: As the students work, ask: **What is peace? What makes a place peaceful for you?** Read Luke 5:16 to the students. (Some versions say, "lonely places." This simply means that Jesus was alone there, not lonely.) Say: **Sometimes even Jesus went to a peaceful place to get away from the crowds.** Read 1 Samuel 16:14-23. Ask: **Who was the peacemaker? How did he bring peace?** Say: **David knew the peace of being in the fields watching sheep. David's life was not always peaceful, but David was at peace with God. David carried that peace with him wherever he went. God plans for each of us to carry inside us a peace that's greater than we can understand. It's a peace in our spirits that can be with us wherever we go. It's a place where we can go to meet with God anytime we like, even if our surroundings are not so peaceful.** Ask someone to read Philippians 4:6, 7. Ask: **How can we get God's peace?**

DISCOVERERS' DEBRIEFING

If you have time to review, gather as a large group and discuss your young discoverers' findings. Ask the following questions:

- **What is the most interesting thing you discovered today?**
- **What did you learn today that you did not know before?**
- **What is peace? What is a peacemaker?**
- **Why is peacemaking important?**
- **Do people have to agree on everything in order to live peacefully?**
- **Why is Jesus called the Prince of Peace?**
- **What makes a place peaceful for you?**
- **Explain how you can carry God's peace with you wherever you go.**

Review the Scripture for today.

Pray, thanking God for peace. Ask him to help us learn how to be peacemakers.

Peace All Around

"A hothead starts fights; a cool-tempered person tries to stop them." Proverbs 15:18	"A troublemaker plants seeds of strife; gossip separates the best of friends." Proverbs 16:28
"Disregarding another person's faults preserves love; telling about them separates close friends." Proverbs 17:9	"Beginning a quarrel is like opening a floodgate, so drop the matter before a dispute breaks out." Proverbs 17:14
"Casting lots can end arguments and settle disputes between powerful opponents." Proverbs 18:18	"It's harder to make amends with an offended friend than to capture a fortified city." Proverbs 18:19
"Arguments separate friends like a gate locked with iron bars." Proverbs 18:19	"People with good sense restrain their anger; they earn esteem by overlooking wrongs." Proverbs 19:11
"Avoiding a fight is a mark of honor; only fools insist on quarreling." Proverbs 20:3	"Don't say, 'I will get even for this wrong.' Wait for the Lord to handle the matter." Proverbs 20:22

Peace Flip

Peace Flip

Romans 12:18

2 _ _ _ _ _ _ _ _ _ _

3 _ _ _ _ _ _ _ _ _ _

4 _ _ _ _ _ _ _ _ _ _

5 _ _ _ _ _ _ _ _ _ _

6 _ _ _ _ _ _ _ _ _ _

7 _ _ _ _ _ _ _ _ _ _

8 _ _ _ _ _ _ _ _ _ _

9 _ _ _ _ _ _ _ _ _ _

10 _ _ _ _ _ _ _ _ _ _

Enemies

Scripture

"For we are not fighting against people made of flesh and blood, but against the evil rulers and authorities of the unseen world."   Ephesians 6:12, NLT

Goal

Learn that the real enemy is not people, but God's enemy, the evil one or Satan.

Learn that the evil one wins if we become bitter, divided, and miserable.

INTRODUCTION

As students arrive, give each one a copy of the Squares page (page 21). Ask them to count the total number of squares and tell you when they've counted them. After a few attempts to tell you the number, say: **There are more than 20.** After a few more attempts, say: **There are more than 25.** The correct answer is 30. If one student counts 30, ask him to begin showing the other students where all 30 squares are. If no one counts all 30, you may show them where all the squares are: 1 whole square; 16 individual squares; 9 squares of 4 units each; and 4 squares of 9 units each.

DISCOVERY RALLY

Gather the students together in a large group.

WHAT'S THE GOOD WORD?

Choose a student to read the Scripture for the day.

THE CHALLENGE

Ask the students if they've ever heard the expression, "There's more to this than meets the eye." Ask what that might mean. Refer to the squares they counted in the introductory activity. Say: **At first glance, we may see only a few squares. But there are more than we first see. This can also happen in nature.** Ask the students to name some animals that protect themselves by camouflage. Fawns, chameleons, leafhopper insects, tigers, polar bears, and others use camouflage. Say: **We might look right at one of these animals in its environment and not see it at all. It's the same when we have trouble with someone. We might think of them as our enemies. But they are not the real enemy. Beyond what our eyes see, there is an enemy even more dangerous.** Tell the students that in their Discovery Centers today they will find out about this enemy.

PRAYER

DISCOVERY CENTERS

1. ANGRY EYES

MATERIALS
two pennies for each student, pencils, plain paper, a Bible

DO: Give each student a piece of paper, a pencil, and two pennies. Ask them to place the pennies next to each other, but not touching, and trace around them to make two eyes. Then they set the pennies aside and draw pupils, eyelids, and eyebrows that would make these eyes look like the eyes in the verse you will read. Read Psalm 6:7. Students should draw sad eyes. Ask them to trace around the pennies to make two more eyes. Read Psalm 18:27. Students should make these new eyes look haughty. Ask them to trace around the pennies again. Read Genesis 31:31. Tell them that Jacob and Laban were having a conflict. Ask them how Jacob felt. Students draw fearful eyes. Read Genesis 31:36. This is about Jacob and Laban again. Ask how Jacob felt. Students draw angry eyes. Now ask them to write Psalm 25:15 on their paper: "My eyes are always looking to the Lord for help, for he alone can rescue me from the traps of my enemies" (NLT).

DISCUSS: Tell the students that the eyes they drew represent different ways that we might react when we have a conflict with someone. Ask: **Has a conflict ever made you feel sad? Has a conflict made you feel haughty? Has a conflict made you feel afraid? Has a conflict made you feel angry?** If any students want to share about a time when they felt this way in a conflict, let them talk about it. Then say: **People often think the other person in a conflict is their enemy. But underneath what our eyes see, there is an enemy even more dangerous - he sets traps for our hearts. The traps are anger, fear, haughtiness, and a sadness that does not go away. If we allow troubles to affect our hearts in these ways, then God's enemy, Satan or the devil, has influenced our hearts, and we will be miserable.** Ask: **How can we escape from these traps?** See Psalm 25:15.

2. BODY LANGUAGE

MATERIALS
a Bible

DO: Ask the students to listen to these conflict words: clash, disagree, contest, argue, cross swords, squabble, quarrel, feud, bicker, struggle, battle, fight, combat, duel, scuffle, war, hostile, anger, rage, fury, revenge. Now ask them to notice how tense they are feeling. Ask them to think of a body position and facial expression that would show a feeling of conflict. Then when you count to three, they take that position. Now ask the students to close their eyes and listen to these words: calm, quiet, restful, still, inactive, motionless, undisturbed, mild, easy-going, friendly, kind, pleasant, gentle, peaceful. Ask the students to open their eyes and notice how peaceful they are feeling. Ask them to think of a body position and facial expression that would show a feeling of peace. Then when you count to three, they take that position.

DISCUSS: Ask someone to read John 16:33. Ask: **What does Jesus say about trouble?** (We will always have it.) Ask: **What does he say about peace?** (In him we can have peace.) Ask: **How is it possible to have peace in the middle of trouble or conflict?** (Our hearts can hold the peace of Jesus, even while things around us are troublesome.) Ask: **Who would people consider to be enemies? Why?** Say: **The real enemy is not people. It's God's enemy, Satan or the devil. He sets traps for our hearts so we won't feel the peace of Jesus. How did Jesus say to fight the enemy?** Ask someone to read Matthew 5:44. Ask: **How can we do this?**

3. THREE KINDS OF CONFLICT

DO: Give each student a piece of paper. Ask them to draw two lines horizontally across the page, separating it into three sections. Then ask a student to read 1 Kings 21:1-7. Tell the others to listen carefully and draw what the conflict was about in the top third of the paper, perhaps a vine or grapes. Now ask a student to read 1 Samuel 18:5-9. Students listen carefully and draw something that represents what the conflict was about, perhaps tambourines or singers or a sword. Ask a student to read Acts 7:51-58. Students draw something that this conflict was about, perhaps a cross or angels. Now ask the students to write "Possessions" in the first section, "Needs" in the second section, and "Beliefs" in the third section.

MATERIALS

paper, crayons or markers, a Bible

DISCUSS: Tell the students that most conflicts are over one of these three things. Ask: **What possession was at the center of the conflict between Ahab and Naboth?** (A vineyard.) Ask: **What need did Saul have that caused his conflict?** (He felt the need to be recognized as the greatest.) Ask: **What were the different beliefs that were in conflict between Stephen and the Jewish leaders?** (Stephen believed in Jesus, and they did not.) Ask: **Who would appear to be the enemy: Ahab or Naboth? Saul or David? Stephen or the Jewish leaders? Is it possible that Ahab considered Naboth his enemy? Could Saul have considered David his enemy? Could the Jewish leaders have felt that Stephen was their enemy? Who was the real enemy?** Say: **It's God's enemy,**

Satan. Satan set traps for their hearts: anger, resentment, and unforgiveness. If any of them fell for these traps, they would give up the peace and love that God had for them. Ask: **What conflicts are going on in the world today over possessions? What conflicts are going on today over needs? What conflicts are happening because of different beliefs?** Students can talk about world events, local events, or even their own lives.

DISCOVERERS' DEBRIEFING

If you have time to review, gather as a large group and discuss your young discoverers' findings. Ask the following questions:

- **What is the most interesting thing you discovered today?**
- **What did you learn today that you did not know before?**
- **How do conflicts make people feel?**
- **Who is the dangerous enemy who sets traps for our hearts?**
- **What are the traps?**
- **How can we escape from these traps?**
- **What three things are most conflicts about?**
- **What does Jesus say about trouble and peace?**
- **How is it possible to have peace in the middle of conflict?**

Review the Scripture for today.

Pray, thanking God for showing us the traps of the enemy. Ask God to help us avoid those traps. Thank God for showing us how to have peace in the middle of trouble.

Squares

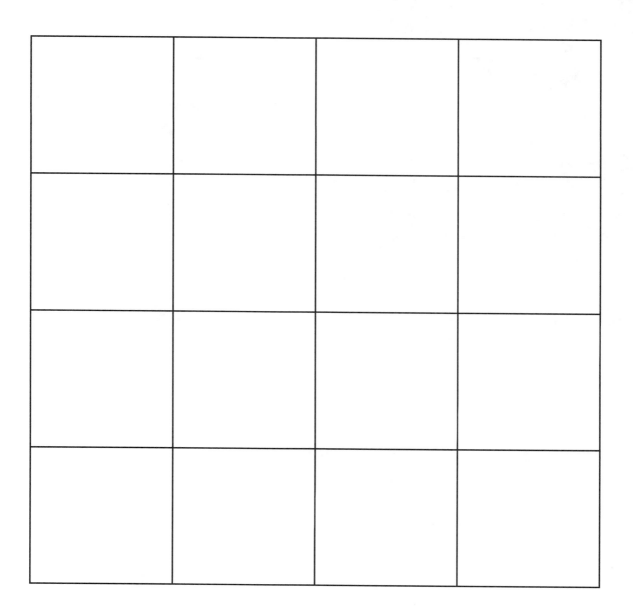

Dealing with Anger

Scripture

"And don't sin by letting anger gain control over you. Don't let the sun go down while you are still angry, for anger gives a mighty foothold to the Devil." Ephesians 4:26, 27, NLT

Goal

Learn how to deal with anger so that it doesn't turn into bitterness.

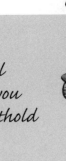

INTRODUCTION

As students arrive, ask each student to find a partner. Then give each pair of students a copy of the Dots page (page 28). Tell them to take turns drawing a line from any dot to a dot next to it. The person who draws the line that makes any four dots a square writes her initial in that square. They are to connect as many dots as they can. The partner with the most initialed squares wins.

DISCOVERY RALLY

Gather the students together in a large group.

WHAT'S THE GOOD WORD?

Choose a student to read the Scripture for the day.

THE CHALLENGE

Refer to the game of Dots that the students just played. Say: **People playing against you in a game are often called "opponents."** Ask for examples of opponents in real life: people who are against others. Ask: **What kinds of feelings do people have toward their opponents?** Then tell them the story of Frank:

> When Frank was just a baby, Frank's father left his mother and married someone else. Although Frank saw his father once in awhile as he was growing up, he never felt close to his father. He never felt like his father loved him or wanted him. Frank was angry. Years went by. Frank grew up. His father grew old and died. Frank was still angry at him. Then Frank grew old. When Frank was 80 years old, he was invited to a family reunion for his father's family. When Frank came to the reunion, he was still angry. All he could talk about was how his father had left his mother almost 80 years ago. Frank couldn't smile. He couldn't enjoy the party. He was no fun to be around. Frank's anger had turned into bitterness.

Ask: **Now that you've heard Frank's story, what do you think "bitterness" is?** Say: **Bitterness is anger that has grown roots deep into someone's heart and makes them miserable. Bitterness grows in hearts that won't forgive. Other words for "bitter" could include: resentful, sour, harsh, unkind, and mean.**

Tell the students that in their Discovery Centers today they will learn more about anger and bitterness.

PRAYER

DISCOVERY CENTERS

1. FRUITS AND ROOTS

MATERIALS
large pieces of manila paper, markers or crayons, plain round stickers of any color except white, a Bible

DO: Give each student a piece of manila paper. Ask students to turn the paper so that the long edges are the sides and the short edges are top and bottom. Ask them to draw a line across the paper about one-third of the way up from the bottom. Direct them to draw the trunk of a tree in the center of the paper above the line. They should draw the tree's roots going down below the line. Across the bottom of the paper, they write, "Roots of Bitterness." Now ask them to draw four branches growing out of the tree trunk. On these branches they can stick the round stickers to make fruit. Ask them to write under one branch, "Get Depressed." Under another, they write, "Attack." Under a third branch, they write, "Escape." Under a fourth, they write, "Criticize." You may want to write these words on a poster yourself so that students can see the words and copy them. They can then draw leaves, dirt, and grass while you lead the discussion.

DISCUSS: Review the Challenge by saying: **Bitterness is anger that has grown roots into someone's heart and makes them miserable.** Ask someone to read Hebrews 12:15. Say: **Roots grow fruit.** Ask: **What's the fruit on this tree? What is depression?** Say: **Depression is a deep sadness that drains a person's energy. Depression is anger turned inward toward yourself.** Ask: **What is attack?** Say: **That's when someone is aggressive with his anger. He really doesn't care about others. He may be loud or seem brave. He may be a bully. He is probably covering up for his own anger at being hurt himself.** Ask: **What is escape?** Say: **Escape is running away from your problems, not facing your anger, "stuffing it" inside.** Ask: **How do people try to escape from their problems?** Say: **Some people watch lots of TV or videos, play lots of video games, or spend lots of time on the internet. Some people try to feel better by eating too much, or by smoking or by having sex or by taking drugs.** Ask: **What is criticizing?** Say: **It's judging other people, trying to make yourself feel better by putting**

others down or "dissing" (disrespecting) people. Ask: **Do any of these things get rid of the anger? No, these things make the anger grow deeper and more bitter.** Refer to the Scripture for today. Ask: **How could these things give a foothold to the devil?**

2. SEEING RED

MATERIALS
plain white paper, dark green construction paper, a pencil, scissors, tape, markers, a Bible

DO: Give each student a piece of white paper, a piece of green paper, a pencil, and a pair of scissors. Ask students to fold the green paper in half and draw half of a heart as shown. Then they cut through both layers of paper along the line they drew. They unfold the green heart and tape it to the center of their white paper. Now ask the students to stare at the center of the green heart and count with you, "One heart, two hearts, three hearts," and so on through "fifteen hearts." Then they

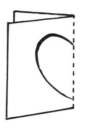 

turn the paper over and stare at the middle of back of the paper. They should "see" a red afterimage of the heart. Ask students to write "'Love your enemies.' Matthew 5:44" across the bottom of the blank back of the paper.

DISCUSS: Say: **One expression for being angry is "seeing red." When we focus on the green heart long enough, we still see it even after it's gone. That's like bitterness; if we focus on the wrong that someone did to us, we continue to be angry long after what happened is over. That's called "bitterness." The way we act is then controlled by our bitterness. How do you think bitterness feels? Does it make our enemies miserable—or does it make us miserable?** Say: **Someone once said that if you hold anger in your heart, it becomes a cobra. What might this mean? How could bitterness be a "foothold" for the devil? How can we keep from getting angry and bitter?** (By forgiving others.) Ask someone to read Matthew 5:43, 44. Review the Scripture for today.

3. "CONTROL ANGER" BOOKMARK

MATERIALS
a 2 1/2" x 8 1/2" strip of poster board for each student, markers

DO: Give each student a strip of poster board. Tell them to write "Control Anger" across one short end. Say: **Anger can be a good thing. Can you think of when it might be good? It can warn us of danger so we can do something to protect ourselves. It can make us think of how to solve a problem.** Ask the students to tell of some things we can do to handle our anger. As appropriate ways of handling anger are suggested, ask students to list them on their bookmarks. Here are some suggestions:

1. Express anger in words.
2. Get away to cool off.
3. Pray.
4. Exercise.
5. Take deep breaths.
6. Listen to calm music.
7. Count to ten—or higher.
8. Focus on finding a solution.
9. Put your energy into doing something else.
10. Draw a picture that shows your anger.
11. Write a letter, poem, or story that shows your anger.

On the back of the bookmark, ask them to write, "'Don't sin by letting anger gain control over you' (Ephesians 4:26, NLT)."

DISCUSS: You may discuss each of the suggestions as students write them down, or you may wait until they've finished writing, and then go back and discuss each one. Ask: **How might you express anger in words?** Suggest that it's helpful to use "I" messages like: "I feel frustrated and angry when...." Ask: **Why might it help to get away to cool off? Are there other ways to cool off? Why pray? How might exercise help? How can deep breaths help? How could listening to calm music help? Why count to ten?** Tell the students that Thomas Jefferson said, "When angry, count ten before you speak; if very angry, an hundred." Ask: **How could putting your energy or focus on something else help? Why might drawing a picture or writing about your anger help?** Suggest that one thing that doesn't help is "stuffing" your anger, trying to pretend to yourself and others that you're not angry when you really are. Then anger can become bitterness, and it will show up in other ways. Review the Scripture for today.

DISCOVERERS' DEBRIEFING

If you have time to review, gather as a large group and discuss your young discoverers' findings. Ask the following questions:

- **What is the most interesting thing you discovered today?**
- **What did you learn today that you did not know before?**
- **What is bitterness?**
- **What "fruit" grows from roots of bitterness?**
- **How could these things give a foothold to the devil?**
- **Does bitterness make our enemies miserable — or does it make us miserable? Why?**
- **How can we keep from getting angry and bitter?**
- **What are some ways to control anger?**

Review the Scripture for today.

Pray, asking God to help us control our anger and not give the devil a foothold in our lives.

Dots

Take turns drawing a line between any two dots across or up and down. The goal is to be the one who draws a line that makes a complete square. That player gets to put his or her initial in the square that he closed in. At the end of the game, the person with the most initialed squares wins.

Peacemaking Choices

Scripture

*"People with good sense restrain their anger;
they earn esteem by overlooking wrongs."*
Proverbs 19:11, NLT

Goal

Learn different ways to make peace.

INTRODUCTION

Bring several sets of playing cards and one clean sock for each student. The socks can be any size, new or old. As students arrive, divide them into groups of four or five. Give each group a set of playing cards and a sock for each player. Students should shuffle the cards and place them face down in the center of the group. Each student should place a sock on one hand. Then students take turns turning over the top card on the deck. When a Jack turns up, everyone tries to slap it with their sock-covered hand. The first to slap it (with the sock-covered hand) gets all the cards under the Jack. Tell the students that this person has found a "foothold" into the deck. Students keep playing until they've gone through the whole deck of cards. The person with the most cards wins. This person can be the first to turn the top card over if there's time for another round of play.

DISCOVERY RALLY

Gather the students together in a large group.

WHAT'S THE GOOD WORD?

Choose a student to read the Scripture for the day.

THE CHALLENGE

Review what you've learned the past few weeks by asking: **What is peacemaking? Who is our real enemy? What is bitterness? How does bitterness give the devil a foothold in our lives?** Tell the students about Elizabeth Elliott:

> Elizabeth Elliott and her husband Jim were missionaries to the Auca tribe of South America. The Aucas killed Jim and four other missionaries. Elizabeth and the others had a choice. They were angry. They could have become bitter. But they chose to forgive. They continued teaching about God. Three years later, some of the Aucas began to believe in Jesus. Some of the men who had killed Jim even became believers. It was all because of the choice that Elizabeth and her friends made.

Tell the students that in their Discovery Centers today they will learn about some of the choices they have in making peace.

PRAYER

DISCOVERY CENTERS

1. WHAT IF?

DO: Ask the students to sit or stand in a circle. Say: **There are three choices we have when we are in a conflict. We can escape. We can attack. Or we can make peace. Here are some conflicts. Try to decide what the people should do.** Read the first scenario on the What If? page. Then toss the ball to one of the students. The student who catches it must offer possible

MATERIALS
a soft ball or a ball of crumpled newspaper, one copy of What If? (page 33), a Bible

solutions to the conflict. If he can't think of anything, he may call on one of the other students to counsel him. Then he tosses the ball to someone else. You read the second scenario. The student with the ball offers possible solutions. Continue in this way, stopping in time to have a discussion.

DISCUSS: Refer to the Scripture for today: "People with good sense restrain their anger; they earn esteem by overlooking wrongs" (Proverbs 19:11, NLT). Ask: **What does this verse say to do in order to make peace? What does it mean to "overlook" wrongs? What else can we do to make peace?** (Pray for the people in the conflict. Discuss the situation with the person one-on-one, or take a friend with you, or take an adult with you. Try to make friends.) Ask: **Is fighting back a way to make peace?** Tell the students that fighting is discouraged by all the experts who have studied conflict. Ask: **Why?** Ask a student to read Matthew 5:38-46.

2. LEMONADE

DO: Slice a lemon and give each student a piece to eat. Ask them to describe it. Now ask them to help you make lemonade by mixing 1 cup sugar, 5 cups cold water, and 1 cup lemon juice. Serve the lemonade. Ask them to compare the flavors of the lemon and the lemonade.

> **MATERIALS**
> a Bible, lemons, a knife and cutting board, measuring cups, a pitcher, mixing spoon, paper towels, paper cups, hand cleansing gel or wipes, and for each 6 1/2 cups of lemonade: 1 cup sugar, 5 cups cold water, 1 cup lemon juice, cookies (optional)

DISCUSS: As the students drink their lemonade, ask if they've heard the saying, "If life hands you a lemon, make lemonade." Ask what that might mean. Say: **It means: try to turn sour situations into something good.** Ask someone to read what Paul wrote in 2 Corinthians 1:8-9. Ask: **Why did these troubles happen?** (So they would rely not on themselves but on God.) Ask someone to read Hebrews 12:7. Ask: **How does God use hardship in our lives?** Say: **Instead of getting sour and bitter in conflict, we can choose to see that God is building character in us.** Ask: **What if you are not in the conflict, but you see it happening? For example, you see a bully being mean to someone. What can you do to help make peace?** (Help the person to overlook the wrong or talk to the bully. Get an adult involved. Talk to the bully yourself. Join with other friends to protect the person who's being bullied. Pray for the bully.)

3. PEACEFUL BEGINNINGS AND ENDINGS

MATERIALS
a copy of Peaceful Beginnings and Peaceful Endings (pages 34, 35), scissors, a Bible

DO: Before class, copy and cut out the Peaceful Beginnings and the Peaceful Endings. Mix up the beginnings. Mix up the endings. Give each student one beginning and one ending. One student reads aloud her beginning and ending. The other students say whether they think the beginning and ending match. If it doesn't match, the student who thinks he has the correct ending reads it. Students can confirm the correct answer by looking up the verse in the Bible.

DISCUSS: Ask: **What do these verses say about anger? What do they say about making peace? Name some ways we can help make peace.** (We could: pray; overlook a wrong; discuss it with the person; take a friend or an adult with you to discuss it.) Ask: **What kinds of wrongs do you think you could overlook? What kinds of wrongs do you think you could not overlook?**

DISCOVERERS' DEBRIEFING

If you have time to review, gather as a large group and discuss your young discoverers' findings. Ask the following questions:

- **What is the most interesting thing you discovered today?**
- **What did you learn today that you did not know before?**
- **What does it mean to "overlook" wrongs?**
- **Is fighting back a way to make peace?**
- **Why do troubles happen?**
- **What can you do if you are not in the conflict, but you see it happening?**
- **What does the Bible say about anger?**
- **What does the Bible say about making peace?**
- **Name some ways we can help make peace.**

Review the Scripture for today. Pray, thanking God for teaching us how to make peace. Ask God to help us make the right peacemaking choices. Ask God to grow character in us through our conflicts.

What If?

1. Jonathan borrows Derek's bike. He returns it when Derek is not home, leaving it on Derek's back porch. When Derek gets home, he finds that several of the spokes in the back wheel of his bike are bent. But even when Derek sees Jonathan again, Jonathan acts as though nothing happened. Derek is angry. What should he do?

    What could Derek do to escape the conflict?
    What could Derek do to attack?
    What could Derek do to make peace?

2. Briana makes good grades. But she overhears Darci telling Stephanie that Briana makes good grades because she cheats. Briana is angry, because this isn't true. What should she do?

    What could Briana do to escape the conflict?
    What could Briana do to attack?
    What could Briana do to make peace?

3. Randy and Brad were both good readers. Their class had a contest to see who could read the most books in six weeks. Toward the end of the six weeks, everyone knew that either Randy or Brad would win. Randy went to Brad and made a deal with him. Randy said, "You've read twelve books, and I've almost read twelve. Let's both stop at twelve and we'll tie!" Brad felt sorry for Randy, because Randy was new and didn't have many friends, so Brad agreed to stop at twelve books. But when the total number of books was turned in, Randy had read thirteen books. Randy won the contest. Brad was angry. What should he do?

    What could Brad do to escape the conflict?
    What could Brad do to attack?
    What could Brad do to make peace?

4. Sharlyn and Amanda were on a team of six students who were chosen to help produce their school's Christmas program. Sharlyn was chosen to be the leader of the team. But Amanda had lots of ideas and was very pushy about them. Sharlyn felt like Amanda was telling her how to run the group. Sharlyn was angry. What should she do?

    What could Sharlyn do to escape the conflict?
    What could Sharlyn do to attack?
    What could Sharlyn do to make peace?

5. Timothy had a part-time job taking care of Mr. Haston's dogs when Mr. Haston went out of town. Timothy was expected to let the dogs out of the house so they could run around the yard for about thirty minutes twice a day. Timothy also fed the dogs and made sure they had plenty of water. In return, Mr. Haston agreed to pay Timothy ten dollars a day. One day when Timothy went to let the dogs out, there was a note from Mr. Haston asking him to bring in the mail, water the plants, and scoop the poop out of the back yard too. This extra work added more time to Timothy's job. But he was still being paid ten dollars a day. Timothy was angry. What should he do?

    What could Timothy do to escape?
    What could Timothy do to attack?
    What could Timothy do to make peace?

Note:

Escape means: to "stuff it" to deny that you're angry, to comfort yourself by eating, watching TV, etc.
Attack means: to fight physically to say mean things to do something to hurt the other person or their property to try to get revenge
Making peace means: to pray for the person; to overlook the wrong (forgiving); to discuss it with the person; to take a friend to discuss it with the person; to take an adult to discuss it with the person.

Peaceful Beginnings

"Short-tempered people must pay their own penalty. If you rescue them once,..."	"Keep away from angry, short-tempered people, or..."
"Mockers can get a whole town agitated, but..."	"Don't say, 'I will get even for this wrong. Wait for..."
"Arguments separate friends like..."	"Those who control their anger have great understanding...
"A fool gives full vent to anger, but..."	"A fool is quick-tempered, but..."
"Beginning a quarrel is like opening a floodgate, so..."	"Never pay back evil for evil to anyone..."
"Don't let evil get the best of you, but..."	"Hatred stirs up quarrels, but..."
"A quarrelsome person starts fights as easily as..."	"Avoiding a fight is a mark of honor;..."

Peaceful Endings

"...you will have to do it again." Proverbs 19:19	"...you will learn to be like them and endanger your soul." Proverbs 22:24, 25
"...those who are wise will calm anger." Proverbs 29:8	"...the Lord to handle the matter." Proverbs 20:22
"...a gate locked with iron bars." Proverbs 18:19	"...Those with a hasty temper will make mistakes." Proverbs 14:29
"...a wise person quietly holds it back." Proverbs 29:11	"...a wise person stays calm when insulted." Proverbs 12:16
"...drop the matter before a dispute breaks out." Proverbs 17:14	"...Do things in such a way that everyone can see you are honorable." Romans 12:17
"...conquer evil by doing good." Romans 12:21	"...love covers all offenses." Proverbs 10:12
"...hot embers light charcoal or fire lights wood." Proverbs 26:21	"...only fools insist on quarreling." Proverbs 20:3

What is Forgiveness?

scripture

"Do not be angry with each other, but forgive each other. If someone does wrong to you, then forgive him. Forgive each other because the Lord forgave you." Colossians 3:13, ICB

Goal

Learn what it means to forgive.

INTRODUCTION

As students arrive, ask them to find partners. Then ask them to play "Rock, Paper, Scissors," but add a fourth hand motion: Heart. The two players face each other. At the same time, each player pounds one fist on the other twice and then makes one of four hand motions: a fist (rock), a flat open hand (paper), two fingers held in a V shape (scissors), hand on heart (heart). Paper wins over rock, scissors wins over paper, rock wins over scissors. The heart can only be used once in play with the same partner. It wins over all. The partner with the winning hand motion scores a point. Then partners pound hands twice and make another sign. If partners happen to make the same sign, no one scores, and they keep playing. Every couple of minutes, call, "Change partners."

DISCOVERY RALLY

Gather the students together in a large group.

WHAT'S THE GOOD WORD?

Choose a student to read the Scripture for the day.

THE CHALLENGE

Refer to the game the students played in the introduction. Ask a student to read Proverbs 10:12 to find out why the heart motion was added to this game. Ask: **How can love cover all wrongs?** Then tell them the story of an airplane pilot who hated everyone.

> He was a very bitter man. One day, a man asked him, "Would you like to get rid of your enemies?" "I sure would!" the pilot answered. The man replied, "Love them, and you won't have an enemy."

Tell the students that in their Discovery Centers today they will learn more about how love covers wrongs.

PRAYER

DISCOVERY CENTERS

1. COMIC STRIP

DO: Give each student a copy of the Comic Strip page. Ask students to draw a story in the squares. The story should be about two people who disagree and how they resolve their conflict. You may remind them of the What If? scenarios that were read last week in Center #1. Students can make up their own stories or use one of these. Post the students' comic strips on the wall for everyone to read.

> **MATERIALS**
> copies of the Comic Strip page (page 41), pencils, and colored pencils, a Bible

DISCUSS: Ask: **If bitterness is holding onto anger in our hearts, what would we call not holding onto anger in our hearts?** Suggest that this is forgiveness. Ask a student to read Luke 6:37. Say: **Forgiveness is a choice. It's a choice not to keep being angry at someone. We choose to be friendly to the person who wronged us. Have you ever heard, "Forgive and forget"? If you are having a hard time forgetting, does that mean that you haven't forgiven? No, it means that whenever you remember the wrong, you also remember that you've forgiven it. So you choose to think about something else, and not to talk about it. The more you do this, the easier it will become.**

2. DISAPPEARING ANGER

DO: Give each student a piece of white paper and yellow pencil, marker, or crayon. Ask the students to write in large yellow letters: anger. Then across the bottom of the page, ask them to write with the pens: "'Forgive each other because the Lord forgave you' (Colossians 3:13, ICB)." Now give each student a sheet of red cellophane or red transparent report cover. Ask students to place the red sheets over their papers and watch what happens to anger.

> **MATERIALS**
>
> pens, white paper, yellow pencils or markers or crayons, sheets of red cellophane cut to the size of the paper, or transparent red plastic report covers

DISCUSS: Ask: **What kinds of things make you angry? Do you have to wait until you're not angry in order to forgive? Why or why not?** Say: **Forgiveness is not a feeling, it's a choice. We choose not to hate or get revenge. We choose not to gossip about it or mention it to others. Anytime we remember the wrong, we choose to think about something else. We choose to be friendly to the person who wronged us.** Ask: **Why is it hard to be friends with someone we have not forgiven? Why does God want us to forgive?** Encourage students to tell about a time when they forgave someone or someone forgave them.

3. LIKE WATER OFF A DUCK

MATERIALS

wax paper cut into 15" lengths, scissors, a ruler, permanent markers, paper fasteners (brads), a pitcher of water, a large bowl, paper towels, a Bible

DO: Give each student a 15" length of wax paper. Ask students to fold the paper accordion-style into 3" panels. They may look at the ruler to see how wide three inches is. Show students how to draw a feather shape along the folded wax paper. They should stick a paper fastener through all layers of paper. Then they cut out the feather through all layers. Next they fringe the feathers by cutting through all layers. Now students gently separate the feathers, fanning them out from the paper fastener. Let each student in turn hold the feathers over the bowl. Pour a bit of water over the feathers to see what happens.

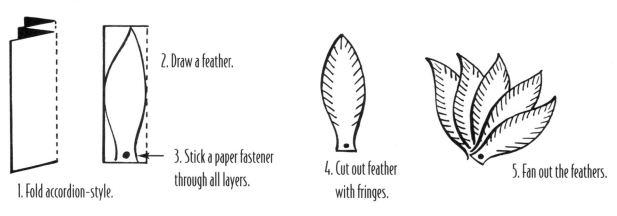

1. Fold accordion-style.
2. Draw a feather.
3. Stick a paper fastener through all layers.
4. Cut out feather with fringes.
5. Fan out the feathers.

DISCUSS: Ask: **What happens to the water when it hits the wax paper? How can ducks dive into water and not get wet?** Say: **Their feathers are oily. The oil repels water, so the water doesn't soak in.** Ask: **Have you ever heard the expression "like water off a duck's back"? It may be said this way: "Problems don't bother her. Anger rolls off of her like water off a duck's back." What does that mean?** Say: **It means that anger doesn't soak in and settle in that person's heart. She doesn't get bitter.** Ask: **How can we keep from getting bitter?** Ask someone to read Proverbs 10:12. Ask: **Is it easy to love and forgive? Why or why not?** Say: **Forgiving is a choice. We choose not to hate or get revenge. We choose not to gossip or mention it to others. Anytime we remember the wrong, we choose to think about something else. We choose to be friendly to the person who wronged us. We let the anger roll off of us "like water off a duck's back."**

Discoverers' Debriefing
Debriefing

DISCOVERERS' DEBRIEFING

If you have time to review, gather as a large group and discuss your young discoverers' findings. Ask the following questions:

- **What is the most interesting thing you discovered today?**
- **What did you learn today that you did not know before?**
- **How can we keep from getting bitter?**
- **How do we forgive someone?**
- **If you are having a hard time forgetting, does that mean that you haven't forgiven? Why or why not?**
- **Do you have to wait until you're not angry in order to forgive? Why or why not?**
- **Why is it hard to be friends with someone we have not forgiven?**
- **Why does God want us to forgive?**

Review the Scripture for today.

Pray, thanking God for forgiving us. Ask him to help us forgive others.

Comic Strip

Two Kinds of Forgiveness

scripture

"Be kind to each other, tenderhearted, forgiving one another, just as God through Christ has forgiven you."   Ephesians 4:32, NLT

Goal

Learn that we can forgive people who have not apologized or are not sorry for what they've done.

INTRODUCTION

Have one small folded piece of paper for each student. Keep these papers in sets of six. One paper in each set should have an X marked on it. Divide the players into groups of six. Each group gets one set of papers. Each student in the group gets a folded paper. Players look at their papers secretly. The one who has the X will be the Opponent. The groups of six students sit in circles. They look at the faces of the other students in the circle, trying to discover who the Opponent is. Meanwhile, the Opponent winks at one player at a time. When a player has been winked at, he says, "I've been forgiven," and he stands. If a player catches the Opponent in the process of winking at someone else, the game is over, and that player who saw the Opponent wins. Then students mix the papers up and begin the game again.

Discovery Rally

DISCOVERY RALLY

Gather the students together in a large group.

WHAT'S THE GOOD WORD?

Choose a student to read the Scripture for the day.

THE CHALLENGE

Review what the students learned last week. Ask: **What is forgiveness? How do we forgive someone?** Say: **We choose not to hate or get revenge. We choose not to gossip about it or mention it to others. Anytime we remember the wrong, we choose to think about something else. We choose to be friendly to the person who wronged us.** Now write "forgive" on a chalkboard, a dry erase board, or a sheet of poster board. Tell the students to look at the word carefully. Ask: **What two words make the word "forgive"? What would it say if the two words switched places?** Write "give for" on the board. Say: **These two words help us understand forgiveness. We *give* up anger *for* the other person. We *give* up our hard feelings *for* them. What else could we *give for* someone who has wronged us? We can give a smile, give our friendship, give them a second chance, or share something with them.** Tell the students that in their Discovery Centers today they will learn about two kinds of forgiveness.

PRAYER

Discovery Centers

DISCOVERY CENTERS

1. NO FUEL, NO FIRE

DO: Place the candle in the center of the pan. Light it. Ask: **What is the fuel that keeps this candle burning?** Now turn the jar upside down and place it over the candle so that the candle is enclosed in the jar. It will burn for a minute and then go out. Say: **Air is one fuel that a fire needs in order to burn. No fuel, no fire.**

> **MATERIALS**
> a disposable aluminum cake or pie pan, a votive candle, matches, a large transparent glass jar, paper, crayons and markers

Now give each student a piece of paper. Ask them to write across the top "No Fuel, No Fire. Proverbs 26:20, 21." Ask someone to read that Proverb. Ask: **What does this verse list as fuel for a quarrel? What else might be fuel for a conflict?** (Rudeness, put-downs, mocking or laughing at someone, bragging, taking the best piece of something for yourself, ignoring people or leaving them out, etc.) Ask the students to draw some logs in the lower half of the paper. Inside each log, they should write one of the fuels they just listed. Then have them color a fire burning the logs.

DISCUSS: Ask: **What puts the fire out? What puts an end to conflict? What if the person who wronged you doesn't apologize? What if the person isn't sorry; can you still forgive?** Say: **There are two kinds of forgiveness: one-heart forgiveness and two-heart forgiveness. One-heart forgiveness is when you forgive someone in your heart, even if they don't apologize, and even if they're not sorry. Two-heart forgiveness is when they apologize and you tell them that you forgive them. Two-heart forgiveness is best. Why? It restores friendship.** Ask the students to think of anyone who has wronged them but hasn't apologized. Encourage them to forgive that person. They may also need to go to that person and talk about it. Then the person might apologize, and there can be two-heart forgiveness.

2. PASS THE FORGIVENESS, PLEASE

MATERIALS
drinking straws, round candies with holes in the middle

DO: Ask the students to form a line. Give each student a drinking straw. The first student in line should hold the straw in her mouth. Hold up a piece of candy and say: **This candy represents forgiveness. Let's say you are all angry at each other. But (the first student in line) decides to forgive.** Place a candy on the straw so that the straw goes through the hole in the candy. Say: **This is one-heart forgiveness. She has chosen to forgive. But (the second student) has not apologized yet.** Instruct the second student to say, "I'm sorry. Will you forgive me?" Then the second student puts his straw in his mouth, and the first student passes the candy from her straw to his. Say: **Now we have two-heart forgiveness. One person has apologized, and the other has forgiven.** Continue down the line with each successive student apologizing and receiving the candy "forgiveness" on his or her straw. At the end, sit down for a short discussion if you have time.

DISCUSS: Ask: **Can you truly forgive someone if they haven't apologized? Why or why not? Can you truly forgive someone who isn't even sorry for what they've done wrong? Why or why not? Why would it be wise to forgive someone even if they're not sorry?** Say: **Because the anger you feel will hurt only you. It can turn to bitterness and make you miserable. When you forgive, you are free. The past no longer has control over you.**

3. EXPLODING CORN

MATERIALS

popcorn, a hot-air popcorn popper, salt, butter (optional), paper plates, paper towels, juice and paper cups, hand cleansing gel or wipes, a Bible

NOTE: If it's more convenient, you can use a microwave and microwaveable popcorn. However, bring some regular popcorn for the students to examine.

DO: Ask the students to clean their hands. Give each student a piece of unpopped popcorn. Ask what makes the popcorn pop. They probably know that there is a bit of moisture inside that turns into steam when it's heated. The pressure of this expanding steam makes the kernel explode. Pop the popcorn, salt it, serve it, and eat.

DISCUSS: As the students eat, say: **Anger can be like that moisture inside the popcorn. If we hold onto anger and resentment, it's just waiting inside until we get "hot" enough to explode! Or it sticks around and makes us miserable.** Ask: **How can we release the anger without exploding?** (We can forgive.) Ask: **What if the person who wronged us doesn't apologize? What if that person isn't even sorry? Can we still forgive?** Say: **One-heart forgiveness happens when we choose to forgive even though the other person hasn't apologized. Two-heart forgiveness can happen when they say, "I'm sorry," and we say, "I forgive you." But we can forgive either way. Why should we forgive?** Review by asking someone to read Ephesians 4:25, 26.

DISCOVERERS' DEBRIEFING

If you have time to review, gather as a large group and discuss your young discoverers' findings. Ask the following questions:

- **What is the most interesting thing you discovered today?**
- **What did you learn today that you did not know before?**
- **What is fuel for a conflict?**
- **What puts an end to conflict?**
- **Can you truly forgive someone if they haven't apologized? Why or why not?**
- **Can you truly forgive someone who isn't even sorry for what they've done wrong? Why or why not?**
- **Why would it be wise to forgive someone even if they're not sorry?**

Review the Scripture for today.

Pray, asking God to help us forgive even those who don't apologize or who aren't sorry.

Joseph Makes Peace

Scripture
"You intended to harm me, but God intended it for good." Genesis 50:20, NLT

Goal
Discover how we can forgive as Joseph forgave.

INTRODUCTION

As students arrive, give each one a pencil and a copy of Word Links (page 51). Ask students to find the words in the verse that link together. The first letter of one word will be the same as the last letter of another word. Students write these words in the blanks.

DISCOVERY RALLY

Gather the students together in a large group.

WHAT'S THE GOOD WORD?
Choose a student to read the Scripture for the day.

THE CHALLENGE

Ask the students if they know who said the words of the Scripture that was just read. This was something that Joseph said. Ask someone to tell briefly the story of Joseph. (**Optional:** Show a short portion of a video about Joseph. The most appropriate scene would be where his brothers sold him to the traders, or where he was put into prison in Egypt.) Now refer to the verse on the Word Links page. Ask: **What is unity?** (It's cooperating, living and working together.) **How did conflict hurt unity between Joseph and his brothers?** Tell the students that in their Discovery Centers today they will learn how Joseph made peace.

PRAYER

DISCOVERY CENTERS

1. JOSEPH'S CHOICES

DO: Use the Joseph's Choices page as your guide. Ask a student to look up the first Scripture reference and read it aloud to the group. Then ask the questions, discussing the choices that Joseph could have made at each of those times of conflict. Talk about what Joseph did: he trusted God and kept doing his best to honor God in what he did and said. Ask other students to look up the other Scripture references and read them aloud. Discuss, using the Choices page as your guide.

MATERIALS
a copy of Joseph's Choices (page 52), a Bible

DISCUSS: Ask: **Did Joseph have reason to be angry? Why or why not? If Joseph had become bitter and miserable, how would that have changed history? How were Joseph's conflicts settled? Which conflicts were settled with one-heart forgiveness? Which were settled with two-heart forgiveness? What can we discover from Joseph's life that will help us learn to forgive?** Say: **Joseph had a heart that trusted God. He knew that following God today and tomorrow is more important than remembering yesterday's troubles.**

2. PAPER PLATE OYSTER

MATERIALS

thin paper plates, stapler and staples, markers, sandpaper, scissors, glue

DO: Give each student a paper plate. Ask them to write across the border, "God intended it for good." Direct the students to fold the paper plates in half but not to crease them. Staple the two corners so the plate will stay folded to represent the oyster shell. Now give each student a 2" x 2" square of sandpaper. They glue the smooth side of the sandpaper to the inside lower part of the paper plate shell. Then they carefully make a blob of glue about 1/2" in diameter on the sandpaper to represent a pearl. Allow this glue to start drying. The top of the glue will be dry in about 20 minutes, but it will still be soft.

Students will have to handle it carefully as they take it home to let it dry completely.

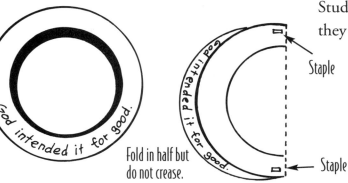

Fold in half but do not crease.

Staple

Staple

Add sandpaper and dot of glue inside.

DISCUSS: Ask the students to tell you how an oyster makes a pearl. (A bit of shell, sand, or grit gets inside the oyster's shell. The oyster begins coating it with thin sheets of the same pearly substance that lines their shell. Layer after layer, they cover this bit of sand. Eventually it makes a pearl.) Say: **This teaches us about our lives. When we have a problem or conflict, it's like sand in the shell. We can let the trouble make us miserable and bitter, or we can trust that God will make something beautiful out of it if we forgive.** Ask: **What were Joseph's conflicts? How did God make it turn into something good? How can we follow Joseph's example?**

3. A CHIP ON YOUR SHOULDER

MATERIALS

a chip of wood or bark, a bathroom size paper cup, a medium-size paper cup, a large paper or plastic cup

DO: Divide the students into two groups, A and B. Each group lines up facing the other about five feet apart. Place the chip on the shoulder of the first student in Group A. He walks to the first student in Group B, trying not to let the chip fall off. He places the chip on the shoulder of the first student in Group B and then takes his place at the back of line B. The student who now carries the chip walks to Group A, places the chip on the shoulder of the student who is now first in line A, and goes to the back of line A. Continue in this way until everyone has had a chance to carry the chip. Now place a bathroom-size paper cup on the shoulder of the first student. Repeat the carrying and transfer process as with the chip, each student trying not to let the cup fall off. Next they carry a medium size cup, then a large cup.

DISCUSS: Ask: **Have you ever heard anyone say, "She has a chip on her shoulder?" What does that mean?** Say: **It means that someone is angry and bitter about something and is ready to fuss and fight with anyone who reminds them of what they're angry about.** Ask: **What could Joseph have kept as a "chip on his shoulder"? Why didn't he get bitter?** Say: **Joseph trusted God. He knew that following God today and tomorrow is more important than remembering yesterday's troubles.** Ask: **What was the good that came out of the conflicts Joseph had? What can we learn from Joseph?**

DISCOVERERS' DEBRIEFING

If you have time to review, gather as a large group and discuss your young discoverers' findings. Ask the following questions:

- **What is the most interesting thing you discovered today?**
- **What did you learn today that you did not know before?**
- **What were Joseph's conflicts?**
- **How were Joseph's conflicts settled?**
- **Why didn't Joseph get bitter?**
- **How did God turn Joseph's conflicts into something good?**
- **If Joseph had become bitter, how would that have changed history?**
- **What can we discover from Joseph's life that will help us learn to forgive?**

Review the Scripture for today. Pray, thanking God for the real-life examples he has given us in his Word. Ask him to help us trust and follow him, forgiving like Joseph did.

Word Links

The chains on this page link two words together. One word ends with the letter in between the chains. The other word begins with that same letter. Find the two words in the verse and write them in the chains.

"How good and pleasant it is when brothers live together in unity! . . .
For there the Lord bestows his blessing, even life forevermore"
(Psalm 133:1, 3, *NIV*)

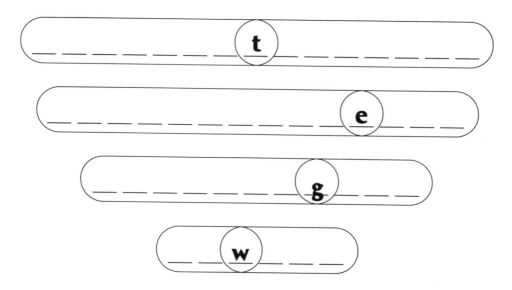

The only way that people can live together in unity is to be quick to forgive each other.

Joseph's Choices

1. **Read Genesis 37:1-11.**

   What was the conflict? Joseph's brothers were jealous and made fun of him.

   What could Joseph have done? He could have become bitter.

   What did Joseph do? He trusted God.

2. **Read Genesis 37:18-28.**

   What was the conflict? Joseph's brothers sold him to traders.

   What could Joseph have done? He could have become bitter.

   What did Joseph do? He trusted God.

3. **Read Genesis 39.**

   What was the conflict? Joseph was innocent, but was thrown into prison.

   What could Joseph have done? He could have become bitter.

   What did Joseph do? He trusted God.

4. **Read Genesis 40:1-15, 23.**

   What was the conflict? The cupbearer broke his promise.

   What could Joseph have done? He could have become bitter.

   What did Joseph do? He trusted God.

5. **Read Genesis 50:15-21.**

   What could Joseph have done? He could have gotten revenge.

   What did Joseph do? He trusted God and forgave.

David Makes Peace

Scripture

"The Lord will decide between us. Perhaps the Lord will punish you for what you are trying to do to me, but I will never harm you." 1 Samuel 24:12, NLT

Goal

Discover how we can forgive as David forgave.

INTRODUCTION

As students arrive, give each one a pencil and a copy of Make Peace (page 57). Students subtract the second word in each line from the first word in the line to get one or two letters. The letters spell words that are the keys to getting rid of bitterness.

DISCOVERY RALLY

Gather the students together in a large group.

WHAT'S THE GOOD WORD?

Choose a student to read the Scripture for the day.

THE CHALLENGE

Ask the students if they know who said the words of the Scripture and why. Say: **David said those words when King Saul was hunting him down and trying to kill him. What had David done to make Saul want to kill him? Nothing. Saul was jealous of David and did not want him to become the king.** Ask the students to tell briefly about David's life. (**Option:** Show a brief portion of a video about David, preferably a part that shows David and Saul in conflict.) Tell the students that in their Discovery Centers today they will learn how David made peace.

PRAYER

DISCOVERY CENTERS

1. DAVID'S CHOICES

DO: Use the David's Choices page as your guide. Ask a student to look up the first Scripture reference and read it aloud to the group. Then ask the questions, discussing the choices that David could have made at each of those times of conflict. Talk about what David did: he trusted God and kept doing his best to honor God in what he did and said. Ask other students to look up and read the other Scripture references. Discuss each one as shown on the guide.

MATERIALS
a copy of David's Choices (page 58), a Bible

DISCUSS: Ask: **Did David have reason to be angry? Why or why not? If David had become bitter and miserable, how would that have changed**

history? How were David's conflicts settled? Which conflicts were settled with one-heart forgiveness? Which were settled with two-heart forgiveness? What can we discover from David's life that will help us learn to forgive? Say: **David had a heart that trusted God. He chose not to take revenge. Instead, he waited for God to deal with those who treated him wrongly.**

2. HARD AND SOFT HEARTS

NOTE: Purchase the hardest sponges you can find. If they are still fairly pliable, get them wet a day or two before class, then squeeze them out and let them dry.

MATERIALS
one hard sponge for each student, scissors, permanent markers, a large bowl of water, paper towels, a Bible

DO: Give each student a sponge and a marker. Ask students to draw a large heart on the sponge and then cut it out. It is probably difficult to cut. Ask why. (The sponge is hard. It's hard to cut it into shape while it's hard.) Let students stop cutting. Ask them to dip their sponges into the water and squeeze them out. Then they can continue cutting. It should be easier with a soft sponge.

DISCUSS: Ask: **What do we mean when we say that someone is hard-hearted?** Point out that bitterness makes a hard heart. Say: **When someone does wrong to us, we have a choice: to become bitter and have a hard heart, or to forgive and have a soft heart.** Ask someone to read Ezekiel 11:19, 20. Say: **Just as you found it difficult to shape the hard sponge with your scissors, God finds it difficult to shape our lives if our hearts are hard.** Ask: **Which kind of heart did David have? How do we know?** Ask someone to read Acts 13:20-22. Ask: **Why did God say that David was a man after his own heart?** Say: **God must have been pleased with the way David handled conflict. What can we learn from David about handling conflict?**

3. A SHIELD OF FAITH

DO: Give each student a piece of poster board. Ask them to make this into a shield. They can cut it into the shape they want. Then across the top border of the shield, they

MATERIALS
a large piece of poster board for each student, scissors, markers, a Bible

should write, "Shield of Faith." Ask them to draw two lines anywhere across the shield to divide it into three sections. In the first section, they write, "God is in control." In the second section, they write, "Unforgiveness blocks my path." In the third section, they write, "Forgiving opens the way to better days." Then they can draw and color designs on the shield in any way they want.

DISCUSS: As the students work, say: **David was a warrior. He knew he was going to be the king of God's people.** Ask: **Why didn't he take his mighty men and go to war against Saul? What are some ways to show our faith and trust in God when we get into a conflict?** (Forgive; don't take revenge, but wait on God to deal with our opponents.) Ask: **How can faith be like a shield?** Ask someone to read Romans 12:19-21. Ask: **What is revenge? Why does God not want us to take revenge? What does God want us to do in a conflict?**

DISCOVERERS' DEBRIEFING

If you have time to review, gather as a large group and discuss your young discoverers' findings. Ask the following questions:

- **What is the most interesting thing you discovered today?**
- **What did you learn today that you did not know before?**
- **How were David's conflicts settled?**
- **What does David's life teach us about handling conflicts?**
- **What do we mean when we say that someone is hard-hearted?**
- **What is revenge? Why does God not want us to take revenge?**
- **How can faith be like a shield?**
- **What are some ways to show our faith and trust in God when we get into a conflict?**

Review the Scripture for today.

Pray, thanking God for giving us the example of David's life. Ask him to help us not take revenge, but trust him and wait on him when we have conflicts.

Make Peace

Subtract the letters of the second word in each line from the first word. In the blanks beside the line, write the letter or letters that are left. Then read them from top to bottom.

If you do this:

f o a m   -   a m   = ☐ ☐

r a i l   -   a i l   = ☐

g l o w   -   l o w   = ☐

p a i l   -   p a l   = ☐

l i v e   -   l i e   = ☐

h a t e   -   h a t   = ☐

You'll have this:

a p p l e   -   l a p   = ☐ ☐

h e a r   -   h e r   = ☐

d i c e   -   d i e   = ☐

c a r e   -   c a r   = ☐

David's Choices

1. **Read 1 Samuel 17:19-23, 26-30.**

   What was the conflict? David's brothers got mad and accused him.

   What could David have done? He could have gotten angry and bitter.

   What did he do? He overlooked it and continued on his mission.

2. **Read 1 Samuel 18:5-13.**

   What was the conflict? Saul tried to kill David.

   What could David have done? Try to kill Saul; get angry and bitter.

   What did he do? He faithfully led Saul's troops.

3. **Read 1 Samuel 23:14 and 24:1-22.**

   What was the conflict? Saul was hunting for David to kill him.

   What could David have done? Kill Saul; get angry and bitter.

   What did he do? He refused to kill Saul. He discussed the matter with Saul.

4. **Read 1 Samuel 26.**

   What was the conflict? Saul was hunting for David to kill him.

   What could David have done? Kill Saul; get angry and bitter.

   What did he do? He refused to kill Saul. He discussed the matter with Saul.

5. **Read 2 Samuel 1:1, 17-27.**

   Saul had hated David and had chased him, trying to kill him.

   Why didn't David rejoice that Saul was dead?

   How could David write these words to honor Saul?

Jesus, Prince of Peace

scripture

"Jesus said, 'Father, forgive these people, because they don't know what they are doing."
Luke 23:34, NLT

Goal

Discover how we can forgive as Jesus forgave.

INTRODUCTION

As students arrive, give each one a pencil and a copy of Stair Step Words (page 64). The students answer the clues to fill in the stair step blanks. Then they will find the answer to the question, "When will the world know that we really follow Jesus?"

Discovery Rally
DISCOVERY RALLY

Gather the students together in a large group.

WHAT'S THE GOOD WORD?

Choose a student to read the Scripture for the day.

THE CHALLENGE

Ask: **When did Jesus make this statement that was just read?** (He said it on the cross.) Ask: **Were the people who killed Jesus sorry? Did they apologize? How could he forgive people who weren't even sorry? Is this one-heart forgiveness, or two-heart forgiveness? Explain.** (See lesson 6.) Ask someone to read Isaiah 53:3-5. Say: **This is talking about Jesus.** Ask: **How did his punishment bring us peace?** Say: **Since sin separates us from God (Isaiah 59:2), Jesus' punishment for our sins brings us back into relationship with God if we will accept this gift. Our peace is found not only in a right relationship with others, but also in a right relationship with God. We can be at peace with God. That's why Jesus is called the Prince of Peace (Isaiah 9:6).** Tell the students that in their Discovery Centers today they will find out more about the ways that Jesus made peace.

PRAYER

Discovery Centers
DISCOVERY CENTERS

1. JESUS' CHOICES

DO: Use the Jesus' Choices page as your guide. Ask a student to look up the first Scripture reference and read it aloud to the group. Then ask the questions, discussing the choices that Jesus could have made at each of those times of conflict. Talk about what Jesus did: he trusted God and kept doing his best to honor God in what he did and said. Ask other students to look up the other Scripture references. Discuss each, using the Choices page as your guide.

> **MATERIALS**
> a copy of Jesus' Choices (page 65), a Bible

DISCUSS: Ask: **Did Jesus have reason to be angry? Why or why not? If Jesus had become bitter and miserable, how would that have changed history? How were Jesus' conflicts settled? Which conflicts were settled with one-heart forgiveness? Which were settled with two-heart forgiveness? What can we discover from Jesus' life that will help us learn to forgive?** Say: **Jesus trusted God. He never let put-downs control what he did or said. He kept loving people and honoring God.**

2. THE PEACE DOVE

DO: Give each student a copy of the Peace Dove page. Ask students to work with a partner. They turn the paper so that the head of the dove is toward them at the bottom of the page. Then one partner places her right hand on the paper, palm just touching the neck of the dove, fingers together pointing toward the right corner of the page. Her partner draws around that hand. Then she places her left hand on the paper, this palm over the tracing of the right hand palm. Fingers are together, pointing toward the left corner of the page. Her partner traces around this hand. Now her partner does the same with his page, while she traces around his hands. These hand tracings will form the wings of the dove. Students then cut out the doves and glue them onto the construction paper. Across the bottom of the page, they write, "'Peace I leave with you; my peace I give you' (John 14:27, NIV)."

MATERIALS

copies of Peace Dove (page 66), scissors, colored construction paper, glue, pencils, markers, a Bible

DISCUSS: Say: **The dove is often a symbol of peace. What else can the dove represent? It often represents the Holy Spirit, because the Spirit came to Jesus in the form of a dove at his baptism (John 1:32).** Ask someone to read John 14:26, 27. Ask: **What might be the difference between the peace that Jesus gives us and the peace that the world offers us?**

- Jesus brought us peace with God: a right relationship with God. The world can't do that.
- Jesus can give us peace in our hearts even when situations around us are in conflict. The world can't do that.
- Jesus is faithful and can be trusted to give us inner peace and make things turn out for good (Romans 8:28). The world may promise us peace, but the world is not dependable. The world often lets us down.

Ask: **How did Jesus stay at peace with others?** Say: **He overlooked the wrong ways they talked to him and treated him. He forgave them. He did not take revenge or get bitter.**

3. CRAFT STICK CROSSES

MATERIALS
large size craft sticks or popsicle sticks, a roll of floral tape, sharp-pointed permanent markers or ball point pens, a Bible

DO: Give each student two large craft sticks. Ask the students to make these into a cross. Now give each student a 6" length of floral tape. Ask them to hold the sticks in place with one hand. Lay one end of the floral tape over the place where the two sticks cross and hold that as well. Then students gently stretch the floral tape as they wind it diagonally around the intersection of the two sticks, forming an X. The floral tape gets sticky as it is stretched and will stick to itself, holding the cross in place.

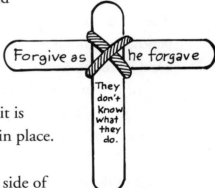

Now ask the students to write "Forgive as" on one side of the crossbar and "he forgave" on the other side. On the lower vertical stick, they write, "They don't know what they do."

DISCUSS: Ask someone to read Luke 23:32-37. Ask: **Was this one-heart forgiveness or two-heart forgiveness? What did the people who killed Jesus think they were doing? Do people who mistreat us and others really know what they are doing?** Lead the students toward the fact that while some people may hurt others intentionally, they don't really know what they are doing. What they are doing is damaging someone God created and loves. They are damaging their own chances of acceptance and friendship. They are endangering their relationships with others and God. They need help. So even in our lives, it is possible to forgive others by praying the same prayer that Jesus prayed. Review the Challenge for today. Ask: **Why is Jesus called the Prince of Peace in Isaiah 9:6? How did Jesus' punishment bring us peace?** (See Isaiah 53:3-5.) Say: **Since sin separates us from God (Isaiah 59:2), Jesus' punishment for our sins brings us back into relationship with God if we will accept this gift.**

DISCOVERERS' DEBRIEFING

If you have time to review, gather as a large group and discuss your young discoverers' findings. Ask the following questions:

- **What is the most interesting thing you discovered today?**
- **What did you learn today that you did not know before?**
- **If Jesus had become bitter and miserable, how would that have changed history?**
- **How were Jesus' conflicts settled?**
- **Why is Jesus called the Prince of Peace?**
- **What might be the difference between the peace that Jesus gives us and the peace that the world gives us?**
- **How can we forgive like Jesus forgave?**

Review the Scripture for today.

Pray, thanking God for allowing us to make peace with him through Jesus. Ask God to help us forgive as Jesus forgave. Pray, thinking of those who wronged us, "Father, forgive them for they didn't know what they were doing."

Stair Step Words

Answer the clues to fill in the blanks on the stair step words. You will find the answer to the question: "When will the world know that we really follow Jesus?"

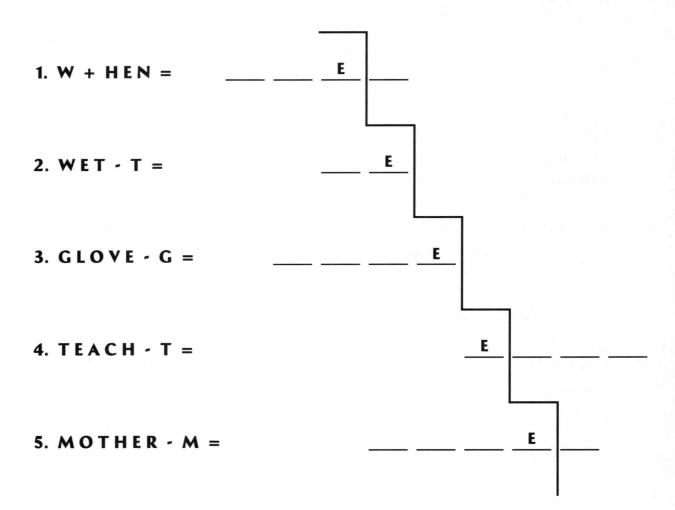

1. W + HEN = ___ ___ E ___

2. WET - T = ___ E

3. GLOVE - G = ___ ___ ___ E ___

4. TEACH - T = E ___ ___ ___

5. MOTHER - M = ___ ___ ___ E ___

Jesus' Choices

---

1. Read Mark 2:13-17.

What was the conflict? The leaders were criticizing Jesus.

What could Jesus have done? He could have said, "You're not so great yourselves!"

What did Jesus do? He didn't start an argument or get bitter; he gave them a good answer.

---

2. Read Mark 5:35-42.

What did the crowd do? They laughed at Jesus.

What could Jesus have done? Get angry, laugh at them, get bitter.

What did Jesus do? He sent them out.

(Sometimes separating ourselves from those who are causing trouble is enough to bring peace.)

---

3. Read Mark 6:7-11.

What conflict was Jesus talking about? People who would not welcome or listen to them.

What could the disciples do about them? They could be rude or put them down. They could take their anger with them and become bitter.

What did Jesus tell them to do? Shake the dust off. Forget about it.

(Sometimes when people don't welcome us or listen to us, or don't choose us for their team, or mistreat us in some way, we can follow Jesus' advice and "shake it off." Refuse to get angry and bitter. Overlook it. Forget it.)

---

4. Read Mark 8:11-13.

What was the conflict? The leaders were trying to start an argument.

What could Jesus have done? He could have argued, fought, been rude.

What did Jesus do? He refused to argue or prove himself. He left.

---

5. Read Matthew 26:47-54.

What was the conflict? Jesus was being arrested.

What could Jesus have done? Called thousands of angels to rescue him.

What did Jesus do? He allowed himself to be arrested. He did not fight back. He allowed himself to be mocked, beaten and killed, and he prayed, "Father, forgive them; they don't know what they're doing."

The Peace Dove

When You Need to Confront

Scripture

"A gentle answer turns away wrath, but harsh words stir up anger."
Proverbs 15:1, NLT

Goal

Learn when and how to confront someone.

INTRODUCTION

As the students arrive, give each one a pencil and a copy of Number Cipher (page 72). Students use the letters in the grid to decode the message which is part of the Scripture for today.

Discovery Rally

DISCOVERY RALLY

Gather the students together in a large group.

WHAT'S THE GOOD WORD?

Choose a student to read the Scripture for the day.

THE CHALLENGE

Ask the students what their coded message said. Then tell them the true story of Katie:

> Katie studied hard and made the best grades in her class at school. But Brooke was jealous of her. In fact, Brooke was so jealous that she began telling everyone that Katie made good grades because she cheated. Soon the rumor had spread through the whole class. Katie's classmates were not as friendly around her anymore. They didn't trust her. When Katie found out what Brooke had told everyone, she could hardly believe it. She was very angry.

Ask: **What are Katie's choices? What could Katie do if she wanted to escape the conflict? What could Katie do if she wanted to attack? What would God want Katie to do?** Tell the students that in their Discovery Centers today they will talk about when and how to talk to someone about a conflict we have with them. Tell them that's what we call "confronting" someone.

PRAYER

Discovery Centers

DISCOVERY CENTERS

1. LOG AND STRAW

DO: Divide your group into two teams. They should sit at opposite sides of a table. Choose a person on each team to be the leader. Give the first student on Team A the matchstick. Give the first student on Team B the kernel

MATERIALS
a matchstick, a kernel of unpopped popcorn, a Bible

of corn. Team A goes first. When you say, "Go," they start passing the matchstick back and forth with their hands beneath the table. The leader of Team B slowly counts to ten. Then he calls, "Up!" All players on Team A must hold their closed fists above the table. Then the leader of Team B calls, "Down!" All players on Team A must slap their open hands down on the table. One of them will be covering the matchstick. Now Team B huddles to decide who they think has the matchstick. When they decide, the leader of Team B begins calling out names of the students on Team A whom they believe do not have the matchstick. If the matchstick turns up before the last name is called, Team A gets a point. If Team B guessed correctly, they get the point. Then it's Team B's turn. The game is followed exactly like the first round, except that Team B passes the kernel of corn. Team A's leader calls out, "Up!" and "Down!"

DISCUSS: Stop the game in time for a discussion. Ask a student to read Matthew 7:1-5. Ask: **What does this story mean?** Say: **It means that we need to remember that we have faults too. The first thing to do before we confront somebody is to pray about it. The second thing we should do is make sure that we didn't do something rude or mean to them. If we did, we'll have to apologize to them first before we talk to them about the conflict, even if it was their fault for doing something worse to us.** Ask: **How do we know when to confront someone?** (If we can't overlook what they did. If the wrong keeps happening again and again. If the person is putting herself or others in danger. If the person is a Christian who is dishonoring God by the way they are talking or acting.) Ask: **How should we confront them?** Remind the students of the Scripture for today. Say: **We should confront gently.** Ask students to give examples of what confronting gently might mean.

2. TELEGRAM

DO: Seat your group in a circle. Tell the students that they are going to discover ways to confront someone. Choose one student to be the Discoverer. The Discoverer stands in the center of the group. He closes and covers his eyes. Choose one student to send the telegram. This student says, "I'm going to send a telegram to (the name of one of the players)." Then she squeezes the hand of the student

> **MATERIALS**
> messages copied and cut out from Telegrams (page 73), a Bible

on her left or right. The Discoverer opens his eyes and tries to see the squeeze as it goes toward the person who is to receive the telegram. If that person gets the squeeze before the Discoverer sees it, she stands and says, "I got it!" Then give her one of the messages from the Telegram page to read aloud. If the Discoverer sees someone squeezing, that person becomes the Discoverer. But before the game continues, give one message from the Telegram page to the one who was named earlier as the recipient. She reads it aloud.

DISCUSS: Stop the game in time to have a short discussion. Point out that most of the statements were "I" statements. That is, they did not attack, accuse, or judge the other person. Say: **The first and most important thing to do before confronting someone is to pray.** Ask someone to read Matthew 18:15, 16. Ask the students for their suggestions of ways to gently confront someone. Ask: **Do you always have to confront someone alone? When would you take someone with you? Who would you take with you? When would it not be a good idea to take someone with you?** Suggest that there may be times when they would need to confront someone while the conflict is happening. If another person is being put down, it might be the time to speak up right then. Ask the students if there's a time when they could use humor to confront someone. Ask for examples.

3. TALLY

MATERIALS
pencils, paper, a copy of the Tally Board (page 74)

DO: Give each student a pencil and piece of paper on which to keep their score. Set the Tally Board in the center of the group. If you have a large number of students, you may want to divide them into two groups and have one Tally Board per group. Students take turns closing their eyes and touching their pencil to the Tally Board. They get the number of points written in the section that their pencil touches. Then they read aloud the "when" or "how" written in that section. If the pencil touches a line or touches outside the circle, they score no points. They must wait until their next turn to try again. If any player hits the center of the circle, they get 13 points. Limit the play to five times around the group. Then everyone adds up their points. Highest points win. If you have time after the discussion, you may want to let the students play again.

DISCUSS: Ask: **Do you always have to confront someone when they've treated you wrongly?** Say: **No. You can decide to overlook what they did and forgive them. That's what David did when his brothers spoke rudely to him.** (See session 8.) Ask: **When would it be right to confront someone?** (When you can't overlook it. When it keeps happening. When someone is in danger. When it's a Christian dishonoring God.) Say: **The first and most important thing to do before confronting someone is to pray.** Ask: **Do you have to go alone to confront someone?** Say: **No. Sometimes it's best to have someone with you.** Ask: **Who could you take with you?** (A friend. A parent. A teacher.) Ask: **What are some good things to say when confronting someone?** See the "how" sections of the Tally Board and Telegrams (pages 73, 74). Remind the students of the Scripture for today, Proverbs 15:1.

DISCOVERERS' DEBRIEFING

If you have time to review, gather as a large group and discuss your young discoverers' findings. Ask the following questions:

- **What is the most interesting thing you discovered today?**
- **What did you learn today that you did not know before?**
- **Do you always have to confront someone when they've treated you wrongly?**
- **When would it be right to confront someone?**
- **What is the first thing we should do before we confront somebody? What is the second thing we should do?**
- **Do you always have to confront someone alone? When would you take someone with you? Who would you take with you?**
- **What are some good things to say when confronting someone?**

Review the Scripture for today.

Pray, thanking God for telling us in his Word how to deal with conflict. Ask him to help us be wise about when to confront people and how to confront them.

Number Cipher

To decode this message, use the grid. The first number is the row number, the second is the column number. For example, the number 32 means row 3 column 2. So that letter is L. Write the letter in the blank below each number to find the message.

Column Numbers

	1	2	3	4	5
1	A	B	C	D	E
2	F	G	H	I	J
3	K	L	M	N	O
4	P	Q	R	S	T
5	U	V	W	X	Y

Row Numbers

---
11   22 15 34 45 32 15

11 34 44 53 15 43   45 51 43 34 44

11 53 11 55   53 43 11 45 23

Telegrams

I am confused by what happened yesterday.	I've noticed that this is what's happening, and I feel very uncomfortable with that.
Why would you want to say that?	Why would you want to tell me I'm dumb and hurt my feelings?
I get the impression that you want to be respected, and I do too.	I can understand why you'd laugh at me, but I feel hurt and discouraged when you do that.
I feel angry when you talk like that about people.	I think you should back off.
Cool it, man.	I've been angry before too, but it's never right to hurt someone's feelings.

Tally Board

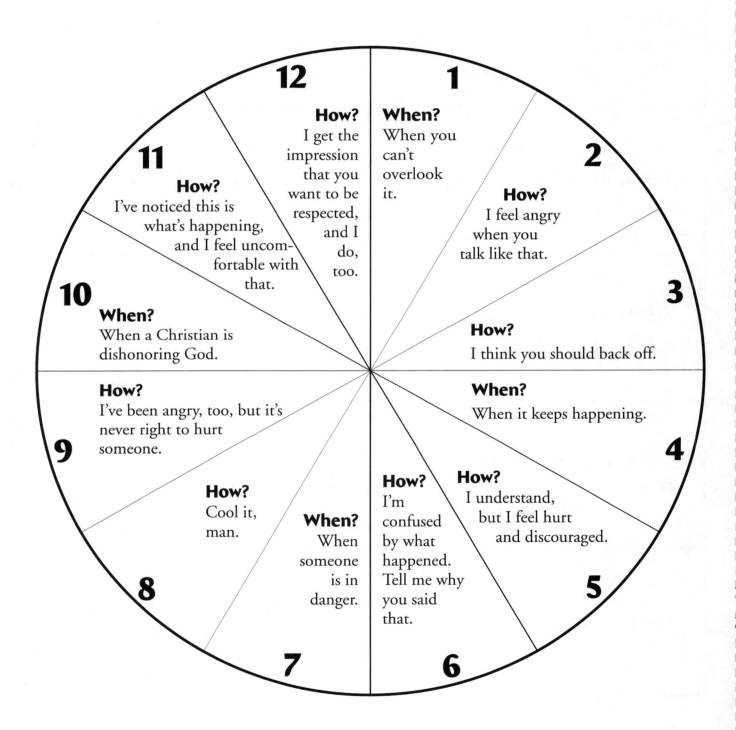

When You Need to Apologize

Scripture

"His son said to him, 'Father, I have sinned against both heaven and you.'"
Luke 15:18, NLT

Goal

Learn what we must do when we are in the wrong.

INTRODUCTION

Bring lots of old pennies, copper cleaner, old soft rags and paper towels, and hand cleansing gel or wipes. Keep back one of the dirtiest pennies to use in the Challenge portion of this session. As the students arrive, ask them to clean the pennies with the copper cleaner by rubbing the cleaner on them with soft towels or paper towels. They continue rubbing until the pennies are clean and shiny. Students may clean their hands with the gel or wipes. Then ask the students to arrange the pennies in order by date. Ask them to locate the oldest penny and the newest penny, and to see if there is a penny from the year of their birth.

DISCOVERY RALLY

Gather the students together in a large group.

WHAT'S THE GOOD WORD?

Choose a student to read the Scripture for the day.

THE CHALLENGE

Ask: **What is an apology?** (It's saying you're sorry, admitting you were wrong, asking someone to forgive you.) Show your dirty penny to the students. Say: **When we do wrong, it's like getting dirty, but not on the outside. The dirty feeling is inside us, in our hearts. That's called guilt. We feel dirty, or guilty.** Ask: **How can we get rid of that dirty feeling?** (We apologize, ask the person we wronged to forgive us, and ask God to forgive us.) Refer to the Scripture for the day. Say: **Also we may be able to repair some of the damage we've done. We may need to replace something that was lost or damaged.** Hold up one of the clean, shiny pennies. Say: **When God forgives us and others forgive us, that dirty, guilty feeling should go away. We are clean again in our hearts. If I pay for something with this penny, and it gets used again and again and again, will it stay shiny? It will get dirty again. It's not enough just to apologize. We have to repent. That means changing, and not doing the wrong again.**

Tell the students that in their Discovery Centers today they will learn more about repenting.

PRAYER

DISCOVERY CENTERS

1. PRETZELS: PRAYER AND REPENTANCE SNACK

MATERIALS

pretzel dough (see the pretzel dough recipe),
wax paper, baking sheet, oven, cooking spray,
timer, pot holder, hand cleansing gel or wipes

OPTION: If you don't have an oven, bring index cards, pens and zipper-locking sandwich bags as well as the pretzel dough.

Pretzel Dough: Mix together 1 package of yeast and 1 1/2 cups of warm water. Let it stand for about 5 minutes. Mix 1 tsp. salt, 1 Tbs. sugar, 4 cups flour in a large bowl. Add the yeast mixture and mix it all together, adding flour if it seems too sticky to handle. Cover and bring to class.

DO: Ask everyone to clean their hands. Give each student a piece of wax paper to work on and a 1" ball of dough. Direct the students to roll these into ropes and twist them into a typical pretzel shape. If you have an oven, spray a baking sheet with cooking spray and bake the pretzels at 425 degrees for 12-15 minutes. If you don't have an oven, give each student a sandwich bag, pen, and index card. Ask the students to write on their index cards, "Bake on greased baking sheet for 12-15 minutes at 425 degrees." Then they place their unbaked pretzels into sandwich bags with the index cards and take them home to bake.

DISCUSS: Tell the students that pretzels were first made in southern Europe. Pretzels were shaped to look like the crossed arms of a child praying and repenting. Ask: **What does it mean to repent?** Tell the students that the word used in the Bible for "repent" is "metanoia" (meh-tah-*noy*-ah). It means "to change your mind" or "to turn around." Ask: **What would you change your mind about? You'd change your mind about the way to speak and act. How would you "turn around?" You'd stop doing what you were doing wrong.** Say: **When some people say, "I'm sorry," they mean, "I'm sorry I got caught." Or they mean, "I'm sorry you're upset at me." That isn't repenting. Repenting is changing your mind about how to act and speak. It's turning around from doing wrong to doing right.** Ask: **Is it hard or easy to repent? Why? Why does God ask us to repent?**

2. STRAIGHTEN OUT

MATERIALS
a Bible, tissue paper cut into sections 5" long and 2" wide, pencils, plastic disposable picnic plates, plastic spoons, a pitcher of water

DO: First ask a student to read the story of the prodigal son from Luke 15:11-24. Ask: **What did the son say when he apologized?** (He admitted that he was wrong.) **Did he send his father a message of apology from the distant city and keep living the same way he'd lived before?** Say: **The son changed his whole way of life. That's more than just saying, "I'm sorry." That's repenting.**

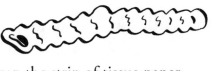

Give each student a plate, a pencil, and a 5" x 2" piece of tissue paper. Tell the students to wrap the strip of tissue paper around the pencil. Then ask them to slide the tissue paper off, starting at the top of the pencil, pulling the paper down and off as if they were taking off a sock. The paper should be crumpled up as it comes off the pencil. Now they lay the crumpled paper on the plate. Give each student a spoon and let them dip up about a half of a spoonful or less of water. Then they drip a couple of drops of water onto the crumpled paper. Ask them to watch what happens. Then they may drip another couple of drops on it. It begins to straighten out. (It won't straighten out all the way.)

DISCUSS: Say: **Repenting is like "straightening out" our lives. It's leaving behind the way we were so that we can do things differently from now on. This paper may not straighten out all the way, but our lives can straighten out all the way. How? With God's help, we can change the wrong we're doing and begin living the right way.** Ask: **Is it easy or hard to apologize? Why? Is it easy or hard to repent? Why?** Remind the students that repenting is more than apologizing. It's changing the way we speak or act. What are some words we can use when we repent? Suggest that we ask God for help to find the right words and the right time to apologize to someone we've wronged.

3. REPENT BALL

MATERIALS
a beach ball or other soft ball, a Bible

DO: Students stand in a circle. Give one student the ball. When you say, "Go," the student passes the ball to the student on her right or left. Whichever direction the ball is passed, it keeps going around the circle in that direction until you call out, "Repent." Then the students quickly pass the ball in the other direction. Every time you call, "Repent," the ball changes direction. After a few minutes playing the game this way, tell the students to stop. Tell the students they can now throw the ball across the circle to anyone they want, but they must pay close attention to the person who threw them the ball, because when you say, "Repent," the ball changes direction and is now thrown back the same way it came. In other words, you throw the ball to the person who threw you the ball. Play the game in this way for awhile, and then sit for a discussion.

DISCUSS: Ask: **What does it mean to repent?** (It means to change direction.) Ask a student to read Jeremiah 8:4-7. Ask: **Have you ever been riding in a car or van when the driver went the wrong direction? What happened?** (They had to turn around.) **Why? So they could get to where they were going.** Say: **Repentance is like that. We discover that we're going the wrong direction in life, because we've acted or said something that was sinful.** Ask: **How is repentance different than just apologizing? Apologizing is part of repentance, but to repent you must change the way you are living. You must change your mind and your heart about what's right and wrong. You must "turn around." It may even include making restitution: replacing something that was damaged, or making up for what you did wrong.** Ask someone to read Isaiah 57:15. If your version says, "contrite" or "broken" hearts, tell students that this means a heart that is repenting. Ask: **What does God promise for contrite, broken, repenting hearts? Why would God want us to apologize to someone? Is it easy to apologize? Why or why not? What might give you the courage to apologize?** Suggest that we first repent to God and then ask him to give us the courage and the words to apologize to someone else.

DISCOVERERS' DEBRIEFING

Discoverers' Debriefin Debriefing

If you have time to review, gather as a large group and discuss your young discoverers' findings. Ask the following questions:

- **What is the most interesting thing you discovered today?**
- **What did you learn today that you did not know before?**
- **What does it mean to repent?**
- **How is repentance different than just apologizing?**
- **Is it hard or easy to repent? Why?**
- **Why does God ask us to repent?**
- **What are some words we can use when we repent?**
- **What might give you the courage to apologize?**

Review the Scripture for today.

Pray, thanking God for showing us how to repent. Thank him for forgiving us. Ask God to help us have the courage to apologize. Ask him to help us truly repent and change when we've done wrong.

Seventy Times Seven

scripture

"Then Peter came to him (Jesus) and asked, 'Lord, how often should I forgive someone who sins against me? Seven times?' 'No!' Jesus replied, 'seventy times seven!'" *Matthew 18:21, 22, NLT*

Goal

Learn that God wants us to live with hearts that continually forgive.

INTRODUCTION

As students arrive, give each one an index card and pencil. Ask them to think of something that seems peaceful to them: a nap on Sunday afternoon, a picnic, a sunset, a snowy day, a fire in the fireplace, a starry sky, a still pond, etc. Then they should write a riddle of that thing on their card. The riddle would consist of descriptive clues, but would not name the thing they thought of. As students finish their clues, number them. Post them on the wall, or line them up on a table. Then give each student a sheet of paper. They read the riddles, writing on their papers the number of the riddle and their guess for what the riddle is talking about.

DISCOVERY RALLY

Gather the students together in a large group.

WHAT'S THE GOOD WORD?

Choose a student to read the Scripture for the day.

THE CHALLENGE

Write the equation "70 x 7 =" on a board. Ask the students to figure out how many seventy times seven really is. Ask: **Did Jesus mean that if someone sins against us 491 times, we shouldn't forgive? What did he mean?** Say: **He meant that we should live with hearts that continually forgive.** Now read the riddles that the students wrote in the introductory activity, and let everyone tell what they think that riddle referred to. Say: **People can be in the most peaceful settings in the world, but if their hearts are full of anger and bitterness, they will not feel peace.** Tell the students that in their Discovery Centers today they will learn about living with forgiving hearts.

PRAYER

DISCOVERY CENTERS

1. BEND OR BREAK

DO: Give each student a straw. Ask them to hold the straw in their left hand, then bend the straw in half with their right hand and quickly let it go with their right hand. Now give each student a piece of spaghetti. Ask them to bed the spaghetti in half and let go quickly. Ask them to compare the results of bending the straw and the spaghetti. Ask: **Why did the straw and the spaghetti react differently to the force**

MATERIALS
plastic drinking straws, uncooked spaghetti, construction paper, glue, markers, a Bible

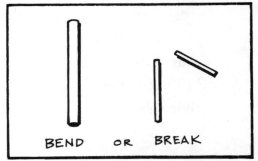

BEND   OR   BREAK

bending them in half? Now give each student a piece of construction paper. Ask students to glue the straw in the left half of the page and the broken spaghetti in the right half of the page. Then they should write "Bend" under the straw, "Or" in the center, and "Break" under the spaghetti.

DISCUSS: Say: **We can choose to be like the straw or like the spaghetti. If someone sins against us, even if they do it again and again, we can forgive and keep growing with God's peace in our hearts. Or we can choose not to forgive. Then our hearts get hard, and we live with hard, broken hearts.** Ask someone to read 1 Corinthians 4:12. Ask someone else to read 2 Corinthians 4:6-9. Tell the students that the apostle Paul was writing this to Jesus' followers in the city of Corinth. Ask: **How was it possible for Paul to be pressured on every side but not crushed? How could he be struck down but not destroyed? He lived with a forgiving heart.** Ask someone to read Proverbs 24:16. Ask: **How can you become a forgiving person?**

2. PUT-DOWNS

DO: Blow up a balloon. Draw a simple face on it, using the tied end of the balloon as the neck. Ask for someone to tell you a put-down that they've heard. Gently poke a hole in the balloon close to the place where it's tied. The air will begin seeping out. Ask for another put-down. Poke another hole in the balloon. Continue in this way as the air seeps out of the balloon. Now give a balloon to each student. Ask them to blow it up

and draw a face on it. Give each student a fourth of a large piece of poster board. Let students trace around the Feet patterns and then cut them out. They cut a slit as shown and slip the tied end of the balloon through it.

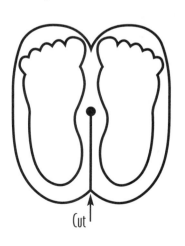

Cut

Slip tied end of balloon through slit

> **MATERIALS**
> round balloons, a few straight pins, permanent markers, four copies of the Feet pattern (page 86), poster board cut into four pieces: one piece per student, scissors

DISCUSS: Ask: **What's a put-down?** Say: **The average student receives 213 put-downs a week.** Ask: **How does it feel to receive a put-down? Do put-downs encourage people or discourage them? If 213 put-downs per week is true, and if a student forgave each put-down she got, how long would it be before she had forgiven 70 x 7 (490 times)? Why would it be important for her to live with a forgiving heart? What makes it hard to forgive someone for doing the same thing more than once? How does God treat us if we do the same wrong thing after he's already forgiven us for it once? Does God care if we keep doing that same wrong thing over and over again, and keep asking him to forgive us? If he cares, why would he keep forgiving us? Why should we keep forgiving others?**

3. DEBTOR

MATERIALS
a Bible, several packets of play money, markers, two copies of Borrow (page 87) with the amounts cut apart

DO: Divide the passage of Matthew 18:21-35 between several students and ask them to read it aloud to the group. As they read about the man who owed lots of money, spread a large amount of the play money on the table. As they read about the man who owed only a little, place two bills on the table so that the difference in the amounts is visible. When the reading is finished, give each student one bill of play money. Ask students to write on their bills, "'Forgive as the Lord forgave you' (Colossians 3:13, NIV)."

DISCUSS: Ask: **What does this story mean in our lives? Who is the King?** God. **Who is the debtor who owed lots of money to the king?** (Us.) **Who is the one who owed the small amount of money to the first debtor?** (People who sin against us.) **Why was the King angry? Why would God be angry at us for refusing to forgive someone?** (Because he has forgiven us of so much. The least we could do is to forgive others.) Review the steps toward making peace. Refer to the discussion in Center 2 for suggestions.

DO: If you have time, play a quick game of Debtor. Ask the students to set aside the bill they wrote on. Then deal out the rest of the money to the students for the game. Mix up the amount cards which you cut from the Borrow page.

Begin slowly laying them face down, one by one, in a stack in front of you. Choose one student to go first. At any point, he may say, "Borrow." At that point, you give the student the card you just placed on the stack. The student holds that card. Now it's the next student's turn to borrow. If you run out of cards before all students have borrowed, pick the stack up and start over. Continue until all students have borrowed. Now the first student looks at the cards that you gave him to see how much he borrowed. He must pay the student to his right that amount in play money. The student to his left then looks to see how much she borrowed. She must pay the first student. The student to her left pays her, and so on. If anyone has the "forgiven" card, they owe no debt.

DISCUSS: Ask: **How is forgiving a debt like forgiving sin? Why does God want us to forgive others instead of getting bitter or getting even? What would make it hard to forgive someone over and over again?**

DISCOVERERS' DEBRIEFING

If you have time to review, gather as a large group and discuss your young discoverers' findings. Ask the following questions:

- **What is the most interesting thing you discovered today?**
- **What did you learn today that you did not know before?**
- **How was it possible for Paul to be struck down but not destroyed?**
- **What does forgiving 70 x 7 mean?**
- **What would make it hard to forgive someone over and over again?**
- **What does the story of the debtor mean in our lives?**
- **Why does God want us to forgive others instead of getting bitter or getting even?**

Review the Scripture for today. Pray, thanking God for forgiving us. Ask God to help us live with forgiving hearts, even if we have to forgive others again.

NOTE: During the coming week, ask someone who plays guitar, violin, keyboard, or other stringed instrument to visit your classroom and bring their instrument. Tell them about the activity in Discovery Center #3 next week, so they will know what to expect.

Feet Pattern

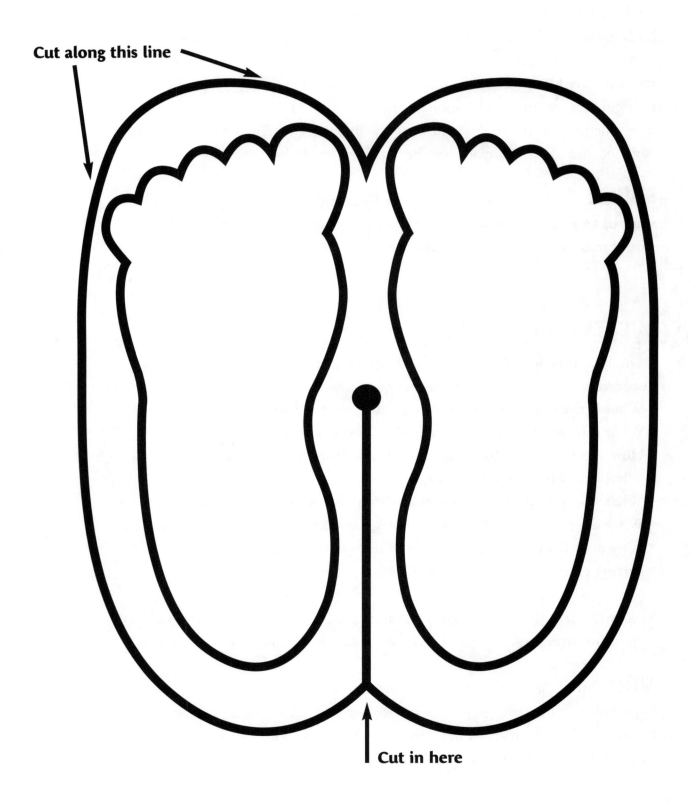

Cut along this line

Cut in here

Borrow

$10	$20	$30	$40
$50	$60	$70	$80
$90	$100	Forgiven	$90
$80	$70	$60	$50

Harmony

Scripture

"Finally, all of you, live in harmony with one another; be sympathetic, love as brothers, be compassionate and humble." 1 Peter 3:8, NIV

Goal

Review the principles of making peace.
Learn that in order to live in harmony, we must think of other people's feelings and interests.

INTRODUCTION

As the students arrive, give each one a copy of Interest Bingo (page 93). Tell them to find classmates who fit the descriptions in the boxes. When they find one, that person must sign his name in the appropriate blank. Each classmate may sign only one blank on each sheet. Ask the students to try to fill in all the blanks in a row or column or diagonally.

DISCOVERY RALLY

Gather the students together in a large group.

WHAT'S THE GOOD WORD?

Choose a student to read the Scripture for the day.

THE CHALLENGE

First, ask the students to fold their hands. Now they should look at their hands and everyone else's. Tell them to notice that some students probably folded their hands differently than they did. Next, ask the students to fold their arms. Now they should look at which of their arms is on top. Tell them to look at each other's folded arms to notice that some students folded their arms with a different arm on top. Then ask the students to wave at you and keep waving. Now they should look to see the different ways that people wave. Refer to the Bingo pages they used in the introduction. Ask: **Was it easy or hard to find people who fit the descriptions?** Say: **Some people are interested in one thing, some people are interested in another. Even the handwriting is different from person to person. Sometimes it's our different interests that cause conflicts.** Tell the students that in their Discovery Centers today they will learn how paying attention to the interests of others can help make peace.

PRAYER

DISCOVERY CENTERS

1. LINKING DOVES

DO: Give each student one piece of paper and a copy of the Linking Doves page. Ask students to tape the short end of the paper to the top of the Linking Doves page. Then ask students to fold this long strip accordion-style as shown, using the dove on the Linking page as the top panel. Then students cut around the dove pattern through all layers, being careful not to cut the folded

MATERIALS
paper, tape, scissors, markers, copies of the Linking Doves page (page 94)

section at the tip of the wings. Then they unfold the Linking Doves. On the first dove, they write "Pray." On the second, they write "Forgive" and draw one small heart. On the third, they write "Talk and Listen." On the fourth, they write "Agree" with a question mark and two small hearts. On the fifth, they write "Trust God." On the sixth, they write "70 x 7."

DISCUSS: As students write on each dove, discuss the significance of what they are writing. Ask: **Why would praying be the first thing to do when someone sins against us? Why would the second thing be forgiving?** Say: **One heart means one-heart forgiveness.** Ask: **Why?** (Because you haven't talked to them and they haven't apologized yet.) **Do we have to talk to someone after this?** (Only if we can't overlook what they did. Otherwise, we've forgiven them and can go on being friends.) **But what if you can't overlook what they did?** (Then go on to talk and listen.) Say: **This includes asking for forgiveness if you've been part of the problem.** Ask: **Do you have to talk to them alone?** (No, you can take someone with you.) **What kinds of things could you say? Why would it be important to listen? Why would "agree" have a question mark after it?** (Because you might not be able to agree on a solution to the problem.) **What do the two hearts mean?** Say: **If the person is sorry and asks you to forgive, then you forgive them. That's two-heart forgiveness.** Ask: **What if they're not sorry?** (Then you can still have one-heart forgiveness.) **Why is it important to trust God?** (Because he will deal with the person who wronged us, and he can give us peace.)

2. WHAT DO YOU SEE?

MATERIALS
a Bible, pencils, one copy per student of
What Do You See? (page 95)

DO: Give each student a pencil and the What Do You See? page. Ask them to look at it carefully and tell you what they see. Ask them to answer the questions. Then go through the questions, asking them to raise their hands if they saw the glass as half empty. Then they should raise their hands if they saw the glass as half full. Continue through the page in this way. Now ask students to turn the paper over and make a list of things to do to make peace:

1. Pray
2. Forgive
3. Talk and Listen
4. Agree?
5. Trust God
6. 70 x 7

DISCUSS: Say: **Sometimes we disagree because we see things differently.** Ask someone to read Philippians 2:4. Ask: **What's important about respecting someone else's interests? How can we do this?** Say: **One church was building a new auditorium. Some people wanted red carpet. Others wanted blue. They got into an argument. They got so mad at each other that the ones who wanted red carpet left that church and started their own church.** Ask someone to read Galatians 5:14, 15. Ask: **What do you think about what that church did? Now that you know about making peace, what would you tell them to do?** Refer to the list that the students made. Talk about each point on the list as described in Center #1.

3. HARMONY

MATERIALS
song cards copied and cut out from Name the
Tune (page 96), a musician who plays guitar,
violin, keyboard, or other stringed instrument,
and his or her instrument, a Bible

DO: Ask your guest musician to play all the strings together without making any distinct notes. Ask the students to describe this sound. Then ask the musician to play part of a song. Ask the students to describe this sound.

Point out that when the notes fit together in a pleasing way, it's called "harmony." Now show the musician one of the Name the Tune song cards. Ask the musician to play a few bars of the rhythm of the song on one note only. Ask the students to guess what song it is. Continue in this way with the other songs on the song cards.

DISCUSS: Ask someone to read 1 Peter 3:8. Ask: **What does it mean to live in "harmony" with each other? How can we do that? What does it mean to be sympathetic? What does it mean to be compassionate? What does it mean to be humble? Why might these be good character qualities to have in order to make peace? What are some other things to do to make peace?**

DISCOVERERS' DEBRIEFING

If you have time to review, gather as a large group and discuss your young discoverers' findings. Ask the following questions:

- **What is the most interesting thing you discovered today?**
- **What did you learn today that you did not know before?**
- **Why would PRAY be the first thing to do when someone sins against us? Why would the second thing be to FORGIVE?**
- **What is one-heart forgiveness and two-heart forgiveness?**
- **Can you still forgive someone if they're not sorry?**
- **What's important about respecting someone else's interests?**
- **What does it mean to live in "harmony" with each other?**
- **How can you live in peace with others?**

Review the Scripture for today.

Pray, thanking God for giving us peace and showing us how to be at peace with others. Ask him to help us put into practice what we have learned about making peace.

Interest Bingo

Likes soft music	Likes loud music	Likes parties with lots of people
Likes parties with a few special friends	Likes to learn by doing rather than reading	Likes to learn by reading rather than doing
Likes to study while listening to music	Likes to be indoors more than outdoors	Likes to study where it's quiet
Likes dogs more than cats	Likes cats more than dogs	Likes to be outdoors more than indoors

Linking Doves

- -

- -

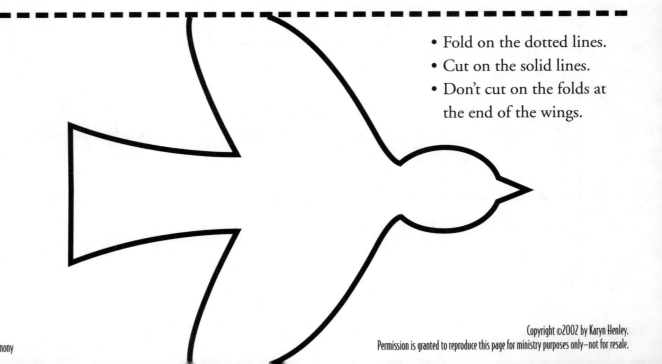

- Fold on the dotted lines.
- Cut on the solid lines.
- Don't cut on the folds at the end of the wings.

What Do You See?

There are no right or wrong answers to these questions. Answer each question the way you see it.

Look at the picture above. Put a check beside what you saw:

❏ a cup half empty

❏ a cup half full

Look at the picture above. If you were the weather person on TV, how would you describe this day:

❏ partly cloudy_____

❏ partly sunny_____

Look at the picture above. How would you describe the man?

❏ halfway up the stairs_____

❏ halfway down the stairs_____

Look at the picture above. What is the boat doing?

❏ moving away from the land_____

❏ moving toward the land_____

Name the Tune

Twinkle, Twinkle, Little Star	Mary Had a Little Lamb
Three Blind Mice	Are You Sleeping?
Yankee Doodle	Rain, Rain, Go Away
The Ants Go Marching	Itsy Bitsy Spider
She'll Be Coming 'Round the Mountain	Jesus Loves Me
I've Been Working on the Railroad	If You're Happy and You Know It